Consumer Education & Economics

Student Activity Manual

BRAND DISCLAIMER

Publisher does not necessarily recommend or endorse any particular company or brand name product that may be discussed or pictured in this activity manual. Brand name products are used because they are readily available, they are likely to be known to the reader, and their use may aid in the understanding of the text. Publisher recognizes other brand name or generic products may be substituted and work as well as or better than those featured in the text.

Illustration: Articulate Graphics

The *McGraw·Hill* Companies

 **Glencoe**

Send all inquiries to:
McGraw-Hill Companies
4400 Easton Commons
Columbus, OH 43219

ISBN: 978-0-07-876782-1 (Student Activity Manual)
MHID: 0-07-876782-2 (Student Activity Manual)

Printed in the United States of America

6 7 8 9 10 HES 12 11

Contents

UNIT 1
PREPARING FOR CONSUMER CHOICES

Chapter 1
Consumer Powers and Protections

Chapter 2
Consumer Management Skills

Chapter 3
Responsible Choices

Chapter 4
Career Decisions

UNIT 2
UNDERSTANDING ECONOMIC PRINCIPLES

Chapter 5
The U.S. Economic System

Chapter 6
The Health of the Economy

Chapter 7
Global Economics

UNIT 3
MANAGING YOUR MONEY

Chapter 8
Income and Taxes

Consumer Education & Economics Student Activity Manual
Copyright © Glencoe/McGraw-Hill

Chapter 9
Financial Planning

Chapter 10
Banking

Chapter 11
Consumer Credit

UNIT 4
BUILDING FINANCIAL SECURITY

Chapter 12
Savings

Contents

Chapter 13
Investments

Chapter 14
Insurance

UNIT 5
BECOMING A SMART SHOPPER

Chapter 15
Persuasion in the Marketplace

Chapter 16
Shopping Skills

Consumer Education & Economics Student Activity Manual
Copyright © Glencoe/McGraw-Hill

UNIT 6
MAKING SPENDING DECISIONS

Contents

Chapter 21
Food and Nutrition

Chapter 22
Health Care

Chapter 23
Housing and Furnishings

Name_____ Date _____ Class _____

Chapter 1 Consumer Powers and Protections

Directions: Before you begin Chapter 1, take stock of your attitudes by completing the following inventory. Read each statement and check the appropriate column to indicate whether you agree, disagree, or are undecided. Use the space provided at the bottom of the page to write your comments about at least three of the statements. You will refer to this page again after completing your study of the chapter.

Statement	Agree	Disagree	Undecided
1. Consumers have very little influence on what products are offered for sale.			
2. Technology both benefits and challenges consumers.			
3. Government agencies offer consumers the best protection against dishonest or misleading selling practices.			
4. For every consumer right, there is a related responsibility.			
5. A person's Social Security number should be a matter of public record.			
6. Shopping on the Internet endangers consumers' privacy.			
7. It is illegal to print or broadcast advertisements that mislead consumers.			
8. A pyramid scheme or chain letter could make you rich.			
9. The best way to resolve a consumer complaint is to write a letter to the company.			
10. Resolving a consumer complaint in court is expensive because it requires the services of an attorney.			

Comments: _____
_____
_____
_____
_____
_____
_____
_____

(Continued on next page)

Rechecking Your Attitude

Directions: After completing your study of Chapter 1, respond to the Attitude Inventory statements a second time. Then compare your two sets of responses. Use the space provided at the bottom of the page to note which of your answers changed. What do you think accounts for these shifts in your opinions? Explain in the space provided.

Statement	Agree	Disagree	Undecided
1. Consumers have very little influence on what products are offered for sale.			
2. Technology both benefits and challenges consumers.			
3. Government agencies offer consumers the best protection against dishonest or misleading selling practices.			
4. For every consumer right, there is a related responsibility.			
5. A person's Social Security number should be a matter of public record.			
6. Shopping on the Internet endangers consumers' privacy.			
7. It is illegal to print or broadcast advertisements that mislead consumers.			
8. A pyramid scheme or chain letter could make you rich.			
9. The best way to resolve a consumer complaint is to write a letter to the company.			
10. Resolving a consumer complaint in court is expensive because it requires the services of an attorney.			

Answers changed: _____

Why? _____

_____

_____

_____

_____

_____

Consumer Education & Economics Student Activity Manual
Copyright © Glencoe/McGraw-Hill

Chapter 1 Consumer Powers and Protections    Study Guide

Directions: As you read Chapter 1, answer the following questions. Later you can use this study guide to review chapter information.

Section 1.1 The Power of Consumers

1. What are the three economic roles that most people play? _____
_____

2. How do consumer purchasing decisions influence the marketplace? _____
_____
_____

3. What do retailers strive to do in order to please their customers? _____
_____
_____

4. How has technology changed the marketplace? _____
_____
_____
_____
_____

5. Summarize the characteristics that effective consumers need. _____
_____
_____
_____

Section 1.2 Protecting Consumers' Rights

6. What do consumer advocates do on behalf of consumers? _____
_____
_____

7. Which consumer advocate inspired many environmental laws? _____

8. What does the right to redress grant to consumers? _____
_____
_____
_____

(Continued on next page)

9. How does the Federal Trade Commission (FTC) protect consumer rights? _____
_____
_____
_____

10. Which federal agency oversees telecommunications products and services? _____
_____
_____

11. How does the Consumers Union protect consumers? _____
_____
_____

12. What are the functions of corporate consumer affairs departments? _____
_____
_____
_____

13. How do the media help consumers when a hazardous product is recalled? _____
_____
_____
_____
_____

Section 1.3 Safeguarding Your Privacy

14. What is identity theft? Why is it a threat? _____
_____
_____
_____

15. Why should you avoid giving out your Social Security number except when absolutely necessary?
_____
_____
_____

16. Whom should you inform if you suspect that someone has "stolen" your identity? _____
_____
_____
_____

Chapter 1 Consumer Powers and Protections

17. Why would a catalog company keep your name and purchasing history in its database? _____
_____
_____

18. What does the Financial Services Modernization Act require companies involved in financial
activities to do? _____
_____
_____
_____

19. What is online profiling? How can you prevent being profiled in this way? _____
_____
_____
_____
_____
_____
_____

Section 1.4 Recognizing Deception and Fraud

20. Explain how the practice known as bait and switch works. _____
_____
_____
_____
_____

21. Why are pyramid schemes fraudulent? _____
_____
_____
_____

22. Why do chain letters always collapse in the end? _____
_____
_____

23. Why should you report any incident that you suspect involves deception or fraud? _____
_____
_____
_____

(Continued on next page)

Section 1.5 Resolving Consumer Problems

24. What actions do you need to take before registering a complaint about a faulty product or
service? _____

_____

_____

25. What should you do if your initial contact about a complaint is by phone? _____

_____

_____

26. What items should you enclose with a formal letter of complaint? _____

_____

_____

_____

27. How does mediation help people resolve a dispute? _____

_____

_____

28. If you agree to binding arbitration, what are you agreeing to? _____

_____

_____

_____

29. What are your three options for taking legal action? _____

_____

_____

30. In what circumstances might people file a class action suit? _____

_____

_____

_____

Consumer Education & Economics Student Activity Manual
Copyright © Glencoe/McGraw-Hill

Chapter 1 Consumer Powers and Protections

 **Activity**

Rights and Responsibilities

Directions: Read the following story and answer the questions that follow.

Mr. Samsoe wanted to buy a small gas grill—the kind with folding legs that can be placed on a table-top or on a stand. He found just the thing at a discount store that dealt mainly in imports. "Portable Gas Grill," the package said in bold letters, and in smaller print, "For outdoor use only." The quality, Mr. Samsoe knew, was not the best, but he planned to use the grill only a few weeks a year and did not want to pay top dollar.

By the time Mr. Samsoe reached the house, a cold, steady rain was falling. Rather than delay using the grill, Mr. Samsoe decided to cook his dinner on his screened-in porch. Mr. Samsoe placed the grill on a table, lighted it, and put his meat on to cook. While he was in the kitchen, one of the legs on the grill folded and the bottom of the grill came into contact with the table, which had a cloth on it to protect its surface. The cloth caught on fire, and the flames spread quickly through the rest of the porch. Fortunately no one was hurt and Mr. Samsoe was able to put out the fire, but not before the porch and several items of furniture were damaged.

When Mr. Samsoe checked the grill, he found that the grill leg was defective. "Products like that aren't safe," he raged. "They shouldn't be sold."

An attorney Mr. Samsoe consulted explained the difficulties of suing a foreign manufacturer. It was expensive and a waste of time. He recommended suing the store instead. That did not seem quite right to Mr. Samsoe, but he thought someone should pay for the damage to his house. Reluctantly he agreed.

1. Assume you are Mr. Samsoe. Which of your consumer rights would you argue were violated? Support your choices.

   _____

   _____

   _____

   _____

   _____

   _____

   _____

   _____

   _____

   _____

   _____

   _____

(Continued on next page)

2. Assume you represent the discount store. Which consumer responsibilities would you argue Mr. Samsoe ignored? Support your choices.

_____

_____

_____

_____

_____

_____

_____

_____

_____

_____

_____

_____

3. What action(s) would you recommend Mr. Samsoe take? Why? _____

_____

_____

_____

_____

_____

_____

_____

_____

_____

_____

_____

_____

_____

_____

Chapter 1 Consumer Powers and Protections

Activity

Which Agency?

Directions: Read the consumer problems described below. Then identify the federal agency responsible for investigating them.

1. In the last year in your community, there have been three accidents (one of them fatal) involving Shooting Stars, a lawn game sold locally at a number of toy stores. The game's packaging proclaims that Shooting Stars "promotes healthy outdoor activity and is fun for the whole family." An enclosed circular, however, advises that children should not use the product without adult supervision and cautions that the game's weighted projectiles should never be hurled at anything other than the "galaxy rings" provided for that purpose. (Violation of these warnings resulted in the one fatality.) Concerned parents' groups want Shooting Stars removed from store shelves now before any more injuries or deaths occur.

   Federal agency: _____

2. The hamburgers are a big hit at the backyard cookout. The next day, however, everyone who ate a burger is ill. You think the meat may have been contaminated and should be recalled.

   Federal agency: _____

3. You prepare a bag of frozen vegetable and sauce mix. When you take your first bite, it has a gritty texture. You examine the rest of the vegetables and discover what appears to be sand or dirt in the mixture. You think someone should investigate any food processor who allows such contamination.

   Federal agency: _____

4. You are allergic to lanolin. When your hands, neck, and scalp break out in a rash, all evidence points to a new hair rinse as the culprit. You reread the label: no lanolin. You are sure it must be there, though. You have all the symptoms.

   Federal agency: _____

5. Your cousin ordered a "bodybuilding kit" he read about in a magazine ad. The ad stated that users of the kit could double or triple their strength in record time and showed photographs of an adult bodybuilder. Your cousin paid $80 for the kit, which consisted of a series of pamphlets describing an exercise program, three cans of a dietary supplement, and a weightlifting belt. He's been using these items for six months with nothing like the results pictured in the ad.

   Federal agency: _____

6. A recent long-distance bill included several charges for calls that you're sure you didn't make. You called the phone company's customer service department, and the representative promised to remove the charges from your bill. After three months, your bills still show a past-due amount for the disputed calls, plus late payment fees. You've written to the company twice but don't seem to be getting anywhere in resolving the dispute.

   Federal agency: _____

7. The contents label of your new suit says 80% wool, but you don't believe it. The fabric wrinkles too easily, and the jacket is losing its shape after only three wearings.

   Federal agency: _____

Activity ## Chapter 1 Consumer Powers and Protections

Deceptive Deals

Directions: Imagine that as a magazine columnist, you respond to questions from teens and young adults about consumer situations they've encountered. Respond to the questions below in the space provided. If necessary, use another sheet of paper.

1. While we were on vacation, my family was given free tickets to a water park just for looking at some vacation villas that are being built about 10 miles outside of the town. It seemed like a good deal—a lot cheaper than staying in a hotel—and you get to stay there once a year. The man told my parents that the special offer was good for that one day only. After they refused to buy, the salesman wasn't very friendly at all. My stepdad told us he didn't like the salesperson's approach. Do you think we missed our chance?

_____

_____

_____

2. I'm looking for a good, solid career and have seen an ad for a company that helps you get a job with the U.S. Postal Service. The only fee is $50. I have the $50 to spare, but my girlfriend is trying to talk me out of sending it. What do you think?_____

_____

_____

3. Our trees needed to be trimmed, so it seemed like a great coincidence when a young guy came to the door and offered to do the job for $40. My mom paid him, and then we left for an appointment. When we came home, there was a branch crushing our neighbors' fence! My mom couldn't contact the tree trimmer because his business card just said "Joe's Lawn and Tree Service, Reasonable Rates, Senior Citizen Discount." What could we have done to avoid this mess?

_____

_____

_____

_____

4. We planned to buy a digital camera for Mother's Day, but it didn't work out. We went the same morning an ad was in the newspaper, but the salesperson said those cameras just "flew" out of the store. Then she tried to sell us a camera that cost twice as much. My brother says we won't go back to that store. Do you think we should give them another chance? _____

_____

_____

_____

Name _____ Date _____ Class _____

Chapter 2 Consumer Management Skills Attitude Inventory

Directions: Before you begin Chapter 2, take stock of your attitudes by completing the following inventory. Read each statement and check the appropriate column to indicate whether you agree, disagree, or are undecided. Use the space provided at the bottom of the page to write your comments about at least three of the statements. You will refer to this page again after completing your study of the chapter.

Statement	Agree	Disagree	Undecided
1. Most items are purchased to meet wants rather than needs.			
2. There is no substitute for having money.			
3. Consumer decisions always involve giving up something.			
4. Success as a consumer is measured by how much you acquire.			
5. It's not possible to gain more time, since there are always 24 hours in a day.			
6. Consumers should never buy on impulse.			
7. Social factors have a major impact on the consumer decisions of teens.			
8. Consumers should be skeptical about information from media sources.			
9. It's not possible to find reliable information on the Internet.			
10. The results of scientific studies are generally trustworthy.			

Comments: _____

_____

_____

_____

_____

_____

_____

(Continued on next page)

Rechecking Your Attitude

Directions: After completing your study of Chapter 2, respond to the Attitude Inventory statements a second time. Then compare your two sets of responses. Use the space provided at the bottom of the page to note which of your answers changed. What do you think accounts for these shifts in your opinions? Explain in the space provided.

Statement	Agree	Disagree	Undecided
1. Most items are purchased to meet wants rather than needs.			
2. There is no substitute for having money.			
3. Consumer decisions always involve giving up something.			
4. Success as a consumer is measured by how much you acquire.			
5. It's not possible to gain more time, since there are always 24 hours in a day.			
6. Consumers should never buy on impulse.			
7. Social factors have a major impact on the consumer decisions of teens.			
8. Consumers should be skeptical about information from media sources.			
9. It's not possible to find reliable information on the Internet.			
10. The results of scientific studies are generally trustworthy.			

Answers changed: _____

Why? _____

_____

_____

_____

_____

_____

Chapter 2 Consumer Management Skills

Directions: As you read Chapter 2, answer the following questions. Later you can use this study guide to review chapter information.

Section 2.1 Setting Priorities and Goals

1. What is the first step in setting priorities? _____
   _____
   _____
   _____

2. Identify some common values that most people share. _____
   _____
   _____

3. What is the difference between values and standards? _____
   _____
   _____
   _____

4. How does setting goals help you achieve what's important to you? _____
   _____
   _____

5. What can you do that will help you achieve an overwhelming long-term goal? _____
   _____
   _____

6. List four strategies that can help you reach your goals. _____
   _____
   _____

(Continued on next page)

Section 2.2 Managing Limited Resources

7. Identify the types of resources that are available to you. _____

_____

_____

8. Why do all consumer decisions involve opportunity cost? _____

_____

_____

_____

9. What is bartering? How does it benefit people? _____

_____

_____

_____

_____

10. Identify the four steps of the management process. _____

_____

_____

_____

11. How do families benefit from developing money management skills? _____

_____

_____

_____

_____

12. What are time wasters? Why do you need to identify them? _____

_____

_____

_____

_____

Section 2.3 Making Consumer Decisions

13. What is an impulse purchase? _____

_____

_____

_____

14. List the first four steps of the decision-making process. _____
_____
_____
_____

15. What is the final step to take once you've made a decision and taken action? What does it involve? _____
_____
_____
_____
_____

16. Explain how family factors affect consumer decisions. _____
_____
_____
_____
_____

17. What are fads and why are people influenced by them? _____
_____
_____
_____
_____

Section 2.4 Evaluating Information Sources

18. Identify three critical thinking strategies. _____
_____
_____
_____
_____
_____

(Continued on next page)

Name_____ Date _____ Class _____

19. How can the credentials of an individual cited as an information source help you evaluate the information? _____

_____

_____

_____

20. What questions should you ask when evaluating a research study? _____

_____

_____

_____

_____

_____

21. Identify seven different sources of consumer information. _____

_____

_____

_____

_____

_____

22. Why do you need to be wary of information provided in advertisements and other marketing materials? _____

_____

_____

_____

23. What information should you take with you when shopping for products? _____

_____

_____

_____

_____

_____

Consumer Education & Economics Student Activity Manual
Copyright © Glencoe/McGraw-Hill

Chapter 2 Consumer Management Skills

Activity

Decisions, Decisions

Directions: Read the following paragraphs. Then use the decision-making steps outlined in your text to examine your options and reach a decision.

You used to have a bike—a 24-speed trail bike you received as a hand-me-down from your cousin. You used the bike for school and errands and occasional weekend cycling trips with friends. Last month your brother backed into it with the family car. The damage he did could not be repaired.

Although you haven't checked prices, you think a new bike with similar features will cost at least $300. That amount, while large, is not beyond your means. You have a part-time job and bring home about $75 a week. With that money, you pay for school lunches, recreational expenses, and all of your own clothing. During the summers, when you can work longer hours, you triple your take-home pay. Most of this extra money, however, goes into your bank account for college. Later this year you plan to apply to the state university, where you would like to major in commercial art.

There are other factors you must consider before committing yourself to any large purchase. Your cousin is getting married early next month. For the wedding you will need to buy good clothes and dress shoes. In addition, your parents have asked whether you want to contribute toward the wedding gift they're going to purchase.

1. Identify the decision: Summarize the *main* decision that you need to make. _____
   _____
   _____
   _____
   _____

2. Identify resources and collect information: Describe what information you would want to gather and how.
   _____
   _____
   _____
   _____
   _____
   _____
   _____
   _____
   _____
   _____

(Continued on next page)

Decisions, Decisions (Continued)

3. Identify the options: List as many possible solutions as you can._____

_____

_____

_____

_____

_____

_____

_____

4. Weigh the options: Explain the pros and cons of the options you identified. _____

_____

_____

_____

_____

_____

_____

_____

_____

_____

_____

_____

_____

_____

_____

5. Choose the best option: Explain which option you would choose and why. _____

_____

_____

_____

_____

_____

_____

Consumer Education & Economics Student Activity Manual
Copyright © Glencoe/McGraw-Hill

Name_____ Date_____ Class_____

Chapter 3 Responsible Choices

Directions: Before you begin Chapter 3, take stock of your attitudes by completing the following inventory. Read each statement and check the appropriate column to indicate whether you agree, disagree, or are undecided. Use the space provided at the bottom of the page to write your comments about at least three of the statements. You will refer to this page again after completing your study of the chapter.

Statement	Agree	Disagree	Undecided
1. Shoplifting is a consumer problem, not just a problem for store owners.			
2. Vandalism is often the beginning of crime in neighborhoods.			
3. Having the character traits of a good citizen is an indicator of success in life.			
4. People are born with characteristics of a good citizen; these characteristics cannot be taught.			
5. Volunteers are not needed as much today because government resources provide needed services.			
6. Leadership can occur behind the scenes.			
7. Conservation of natural resources is a recent concern.			
8. Many ecological problems relate to the production and use of energy.			
9. Individuals can do little to protect the environment.			
10. Conflicting societal goals make some actions to preserve the environment controversial.			

Comments: _____

_____

_____

_____

_____

_____

_____

(Continued on next page)

Consumer Education & Economics Student Activity Manual
Copyright © Glencoe/McGraw-Hill

Rechecking Your Attitude

Directions: After completing your study of Chapter 3, respond to the Attitude Inventory statements a second time. Then compare your two sets of responses. Use the space provided at the bottom of the page to note which of your answers changed. What do you think accounts for these shifts in your opinions? Explain in the space provided.

Statement	Agree	Disagree	Undecided
1. Shoplifting is a consumer problem, not just a problem for store owners.			
2. Vandalism is often the beginning of crime in neighborhoods.			
3. Having the character traits of a good citizen is an indicator of success in life.			
4. People are born with characteristics of a good citizen; these characteristics cannot be taught.			
5. Volunteers are not needed as much today because government resources provide needed services.			
6. Leadership can occur behind the scenes.			
7. Conservation of natural resources is a recent concern.			
8. Many ecological problems relate to the production and use of energy.			
9. Individuals can do little to protect the environment.			
10. Conflicting societal goals make some actions to preserve the environment controversial.			

Answers changed: _____

Why? _____

_____

_____

_____

_____

_____

Consumer Education & Economics Student Activity Manual

Chapter 3 Responsible Choices

Directions: As you read Chapter 3, answer the following questions. Later you can use this study guide to review chapter information.

Section 3.1 Consumer Ethics

1. What are ethics? _____
   _____
   _____

2. What are the basic rules of consumer courtesy? _____
   _____
   _____

3. How can you show courtesy in a restaurant? _____
   _____
   _____
   _____
   _____

4. Why does shoplifting harm every consumer? _____
   _____
   _____

5. What is the purpose of copyright laws? _____
   _____
   _____
   _____

Section 3.2 Responsible Citizenship

6. What does the active process of citizenship involve? _____
   _____
   _____

7. List six civic obligations that citizenship entails. _____
   _____
   _____
   _____

(Continued on next page)

8. Why do voters need to stay informed? _____

_____

9. How can community members show responsibility? _____

_____

_____

10. How might you help reduce vandalism in your community? _____

_____

_____

11. What does volunteering involve? _____

_____

_____

12. What are effective leaders able to do? _____

_____

_____

_____

_____

_____

_____

Section 3.3 Environmental Awareness

13. List four environmental issues that pose serious challenges to health, safety, quality of life, and the economy. _____

_____

14. What does conservation entail? _____

_____

_____

15. Identify the functions of the Environmental Protection Agency (EPA). _____

_____

_____

_____

16. What are four actions you can take to reduce energy consumption? _____

_____

_____

_____

Name_____ Date_____ Class _____

Chapter 3 Responsible Choices

Showing Citizenship

Directions: There are many ways to be a good citizen. For example, some people show good citizenship by donating to charities, and some do volunteer work in their communities. Read each situation below, then describe the actions you could take in that situation to demonstrate good citizenship.

1. Your mom must work extra hours to help with family living expenses. _____
_____
_____

2. A new student at school does not know anyone and feels left out. _____
_____
_____
_____

3. Winter is coming and your town has housing enough for only 50% of the homeless people in your area.
_____
_____
_____

4. There is a vacant lot in your neighborhood that is available for a citizen project.
_____
_____
_____

5. There has been publicity about actions of a local elected official, and a recall election has been announced.
_____
_____
_____

6. A local park has become a dumping site for trash. Because of its bad condition, few people go there and now it's considered unsafe.
_____
_____
_____

7. Your neighborhood is becoming run down, with lots of homes needing repair. _____
_____
_____
_____

 **Activity**

Chapter 3 Responsible Choices

Protecting the Environment

Directions: What can consumers do to help protect the environment? Read each situation below, then list environmentally responsible actions you can take.

1. You discover that in an average life of 75 years, a consumer will produce 52 tons of garbage. In general, what can you do to reduce the amount of garbage you create?

_____

_____

_____

_____

_____

2. You have waste products such as lighter fluid, oil-based paint, and furniture polish that you want to discard.

_____

_____

_____

_____

3. You have too many magazines and catalogs at home.

_____

_____

_____

_____

4. It's been a hot, dry summer, and your community's water supply is very low.

_____

_____

_____

_____

5. You decide to purchase products that will benefit the environment. For example, fluorescent light bulbs use less electricity than incandescent bulbs. List some other products that you might put on your shopping list and explain how they benefit the environment.

_____

_____

_____

_____

_____

Consumer Education & Economics Student Activity Manual
Copyright © Glencoe/McGraw-Hill

Chapter 4 Career Decisions

Attitude Inventory

Directions: Before you begin Chapter 4, take stock of your attitudes by completing the following inventory. Read each statement and check the appropriate column to indicate whether you agree, disagree, or are undecided. Use the space provided at the bottom of the page to write your comments about at least three of the statements. You will refer to this page again after completing your study of the chapter.

Statement	Agree	Disagree	Undecided
1. A person's standard of living depends largely on his or her choice of career.			
2. Employers expect workers to place a higher priority on career goals than on family life.			
3. At this point in my life, it's too soon to start planning for a career.			
4. Changing careers is a sign of failure.			
5. Workers should be loyal to their employers and expect the same loyalty in return.			
6. Job satisfaction is at least as important as how much a job pays.			
7. A college education is necessary in order to get a well-paying job.			
8. Most job openings are filled by advertising in newspapers and on the Internet.			
9. It's acceptable to exaggerate one's qualifications during a job interview or on a job application.			
10. Personality and social skills have a lot to do with success on the job.			

Comments: _____

_____

_____

_____

_____

_____

(Continued on next page)

Rechecking Your Attitude

Directions: After completing your study of Chapter 4, respond to the Attitude Inventory statements a second time. Then compare your two sets of responses. Use the space provided at the bottom of the page to note which of your answers changed. What do you think accounts for these shifts in your opinions? Explain in the space provided.

Statement	Agree	Disagree	Undecided
1. A person's standard of living depends largely on his or her choice of career.			
2. Employers expect workers to place a higher priority on career goals than on family life.			
3. At this point in my life, it's too soon to start planning for a career.			
4. Changing careers is a sign of failure.			
5. Workers should be loyal to their employers and expect the same loyalty in return.			
6. Job satisfaction is at least as important as how much a job pays.			
7. A college education is necessary in order to get a well-paying job.			
8. Most job openings are filled by advertising in newspapers and on the Internet.			
9. It's acceptable to exaggerate one's qualifications during a job interview or on a job application.			
10. Personality and social skills have a lot to do with success on the job.			

Answers changed: _____

Why? _____

_____

_____

_____

_____

Chapter 4 Career Decisions

Directions: As you read Chapter 4, answer the following questions. Later you can use this study guide to review chapter information.

Section 4.1 Balancing Life Goals

1. What is a career? _____
_____
_____

2. How does your career affect your standard of living? _____
_____
_____

3. What psychological rewards do people look for in a job? _____
_____
_____
_____

4. List four strategies that will help you balance multiple roles. _____
_____
_____

5. What is the advantage of telecommuting? _____
_____
_____

Section 4.2 Choosing a Career Path

6. What does a career plan enable you to do? _____
_____
_____
_____

7. Why is it essential to build flexibility into a career plan? _____
_____
_____
_____

(Continued on next page)

8. How has the strategy of outsourcing changed the workplace? _____

_____

_____

9. What personal qualities do you need to examine when making a career plan? _____

_____

_____

_____

10. What resources can you use when researching career fields? _____

_____

_____

_____

_____

11. Identify three practical considerations you need to think about when exploring career areas.

_____

_____

12. Which personal skills are particularly important in the consumer and management field?

_____

_____

_____

13. What traits do successful entrepreneurs have? _____

_____

_____

_____

_____

_____

_____

Section 4.3 Investing in Education

14. What advantages do education and training bring? _____

_____

_____

_____

Chapter 4 Career Decisions

15. How do an employer and a student both benefit from an internship? _____
_____
_____
_____
_____

16. How do distance education programs work? _____
_____
_____
_____

17. When choosing a school, why is it important to choose one that is accredited? _____
_____
_____
_____

18. Identify three special programs that encourage families to save for education beyond high school.
_____
_____

19. Name three types of financial aid that are available to full-time college undergraduates.
_____
_____

20. What advantage do educational loans have over regular loans? _____
_____

Section 4.4 Getting a Job

21. What information is included on a résumé? _____
_____
_____

22. How does networking help you find a job lead? _____
_____
_____

23. What is the function of employment agencies? _____
_____
_____

(Continued on next page)

24. What is a cover letter? _____
_____

25. Summarize the things you can do to prepare for a job interview. _____
_____
_____
_____

26. What are some ways you can sell yourself in an interview? _____
_____
_____

27. What should you verify before you accept a job offer? _____
_____
_____

28. What protection does the Equal Employment Opportunity Act provide? _____
_____
_____

Section 4.5 Succeeding on the Job

29. Identify four kinds of interpersonal skills that are valued in the workplace. ____
_____
_____

30. Identify three types of resources that workers need to manage. _____
_____

31. Give examples of ways you might gain leadership experience in the workplace. ____
_____
_____
_____

32. How can you show courtesy and respect on the job? _____
_____
_____
_____

Consumer Education & Economics Student Activity Manual
Copyright © Glencoe/McGraw-Hill

Chapter 4 Career Decisions

Activity

Interview Questions

Directions: You've recently graduated from college and have applied for your first full-time job. You're one of three final candidates for the position and have been asked back for a second interview. To prepare for the interview, you've made a list of questions you might be asked. You want to be ready with honest, positive answers that will make a good impression and help you win the job. Write your best answer to each question in the space provided.

1. Why do you want this job? _I would like this job to help make the company be successful as possible_

2. What specific strengths can you bring to our company? _A unique perspective on art, new methods of achieving goals_

3. What is your greatest weakness? _bees._

4. Do you prefer working as a team member or alone? Why? _Alone, I would fight with others on a project if I envision it to be something other than what it is_

(Continued on next page)

5. What do you do when you have trouble solving a problem? _take a breath, try not_
to think about it for a few minutes and then retackle
the problem

6. How do you react to criticism? _I'm a really laid back person, I take_
it in stride

7. What strategies do you use to help you meet deadlines and juggle multiple priorities?
Planning ahead. organization

8. Do you consider yourself a leader or a follower? Why? _Depends on the_
situation, I will lead if I have to but I would rather
follow

9. What is your idea of success? _pleasing the customers._

10. Why should we hire you rather than one of the other candidates? _____
I can bring a new view on art, a unique way of
getting the job done and pleasing the customers.

Name _Anthony Anderson_   Date_____   Class _____

Chapter 4 Career Decisions

On the Job

Directions: Workers in any type of job often face difficult situations. Read each situation below and the three options that are presented. For each option, check "yes" or "no" to indicate whether you think that course of action would be appropriate. Explain your reasons in the space provided. Keep in mind that in each situation, you can answer "yes" to one, more than one, or none of the options.

1. One of Terence's coworkers, Carol, won't do her share of the work. That just makes more work for everyone else. Their supervisor has not done anything about the situation. What should Terence do?

   a. Send the supervisor an anonymous email pointing out the problem. ☑ Yes ☐ No Why?
      Carol recently hasn't been doing her part of
      the work. Please check into the issue

   b. Meet with other coworkers and ask if they will join him in talking to Carol about the problem.
      ☑ Yes ☐ No Why? _inform them of the issue, and_
      bring up possibilities of why she should be fired

   c. Demand that the supervisor fire Carol. ☑ Yes ☐ No Why? _she isn't doing_
      what she was hired to do, so why keep her here, she's
      just slowing us down.

2. Annette believes she has worked hard and deserves a raise. Would the following actions be likely to help her get one?

   a. Threaten to leave unless she gets a raise. ☐ Yes ☑ No Why? _You shouldn't_
      have to threaten to recieve a raise

   b. Say nothing and just work harder so that her supervisor will recognize that she deserves a raise. ☐ Yes ☑ No Why? _Its immoral. no free loaders_

   c. Explain why she needs the extra money. ☐ Yes ☑ No Why? _She doesn't_
      deserve it if she has to threaten.

(Continued on next page)

3. Gerald has been given a work assignment that he has no idea how to complete. Should he consider any of the following actions?

a. Ask his supervisor to assign the project to someone else. ☐ Yes ☑ No Why?
research some ideas on how to do it.
or get some help.

b. Admit to his supervisor that he doesn't know what to do. ☑ Yes ☐ No Why? _____
being truthful gains loyalty and respect
_____

c. Start looking for sources of help that will enable him to get the job done. ☑ Yes ☐ No
Why? _This helps your education and work ethic._
_____

4. Tanya's job often requires cooperation with workers in other departments. One of them, Mai, has been a source of frustration to Tanya. The two of them are constantly on the opposite side of issues and frequently seem to end up in an argument. What might Tanya do to improve the situation?

a. Tell her supervisor that she prefers not to be assigned to the same projects as Mai.
☑ Yes ☐ No Why? _It does not help get the project done._
if they are both fighting

b. Avoid conflict by going along with Mai on most issues. ☐ Yes ☑ No Why? _____
Inform the boss that you don't wish to
work w/ her

c. Ask Mai why she thinks their discussions so often turn into arguments and what they might do to prevent that from happening. ☑ Yes ☐ No Why? _Talking about it_
sometimes helps.

5. Doug's supervisor has met with him and pointed out a number of ways in which his work is unsatisfactory. Doug disagrees with several of her criticisms. What should he do?

a. Write a statement explaining why he disagrees and ask for it to be placed in his personnel file.
☑ Yes ☐ No Why? _____

b. Accept what the supervisor said without comment. ☐ Yes ☑ No Why? _defend your_
case.

c. Ask coworkers to talk to the supervisor about Doug's good points. ☑ Yes ☐ No
Why? _You don't want a bad work record_
_____

Chapter 5 The U.S. Economic System

Attitude Inventory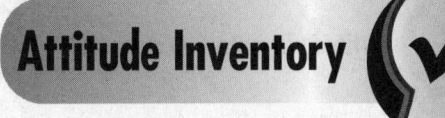

Directions: Before you begin Chapter 5, take stock of your attitudes by completing the following inventory. Read each statement and check the appropriate column to indicate whether you agree, disagree, or are undecided. Use the space provided at the bottom of the page to write your comments about at least three of the statements. You will refer to this page again after completing your study of the chapter.

Statement	Agree	Disagree	Undecided
1. The economic system of most countries is similar to that of the United States.			
2. An economic system can strive for growth or stability, but not both.			
3. In the long run, both consumers and businesses would benefit if businesses simply lowered their prices.			
4. Entrepreneurs get rich at the expense of consumers.			
5. One of the functions of government is to provide assistance to needy citizens.			
6. Social Security is for people over age 62.			
7. Businesses should be free from government interference.			
8. People should not expect government services unless they are willing to pay for them with higher taxes.			
9. Federal, state, and local governments spend their tax money on very different things.			
10. It's fair for people with the highest incomes to pay the most taxes.			

Comments: _____

_____

_____

_____

_____

_____

_____

_____

(Continued on next page)

Rechecking Your Attitude

Directions: After completing your study of Chapter 5, respond to the Attitude Inventory statements a second time. Then compare your two sets of responses. Use the space provided at the bottom of the page to note which of your answers changed. What do you think accounts for these shifts in your opinions? Explain in the space provided.

Statement	Agree	Disagree	Undecided
1. The economic system of most countries is similar to that of the United States.			
2. An economic system can strive for growth or stability, but not both.			
3. In the long run, both consumers and businesses would benefit if businesses simply lowered their prices.			
4. Entrepreneurs get rich at the expense of consumers.			
5. One of the functions of government is to provide assistance to needy citizens.			
6. Social Security is for people over age 62.			
7. Businesses should be free from government interference.			
8. People should not expect government services unless they are willing to pay for them with higher taxes.			
9. Federal, state, and local governments spend their tax money on very different things.			
10. It's fair for people with the highest incomes to pay the most taxes.			

Answers changed: _____

Why? _____

_____

_____

_____

_____

_____

Chapter 5 The U.S. Economic System

Directions: As you read Chapter 5, answer the following questions. Later you can use this study guide to review chapter information.

Section 5.1 Comparing Economic Systems

1. What is economics? _____
   _____
   _____
   _____

2. Explain the difference between macroeconomics and microeconomics. _____
   _____
   _____
   _____
   _____

3. List the economic resources that societies use to reach their goals. _____
   _____
   _____

4. Why must every society make choices about what it will produce? _____
   _____
   _____

5. Summarize the difference between a command economy and a market economy. _____
   _____
   _____
   _____
   _____

6. What kind of economy do most countries have? _____
   _____

7. List the characteristics that are fundamental to the U.S. economy. _____
   _____
   _____

(Continued on next page)

Section 5.2 Producers and Consumers

8. In a market economy, what motivates producers of goods and services? _____

_____

_____

9. Identify the factors of production needed to produce goods and services. _____

_____

_____

10. What is productivity? _____

_____

_____

11. How does specialization improve productivity? _____

_____

_____

_____

12. Identify the three types of business organizations in the United States. _____

_____

_____

13. How can a corporation reward its shareholders? _____

_____

_____

14. According to the law of demand, what happens to the demand for a product when the price goes up? Why? _____

_____

_____

_____

15. According to the law of supply, what happens to the supply of a product when the price goes up? Why? _____

_____

_____

16. How might a pay increase for workers at a company affect the prices the company charges?

_____

_____

_____

17. What are two ways that rival companies can compete for consumer dollars? _____

_____

_____

_____

Section 5.3 The Government's Role

18. What are the four major roles that governmental bodies play in the American economy?

_____

_____

_____

19. Why do public services need to be provided by the government rather than by individuals?

_____

_____

_____

20. Identify three types of benefits provided by the Social Security System. _____

_____

_____

_____

21. What is the overall purpose of public assistance programs? _____

_____

_____

_____

22. How does the food stamp program help needy people purchase food? _____

_____

_____

_____

23. What kinds of government regulations protect consumers? _____

_____

_____

_____

24. What is a monopoly? _____

_____

_____

_____

(Continued on next page)

25. What is the purpose of antitrust laws? _____

_____

_____

_____

Section 5.4 Principles of Taxation

26. For what purposes do governments use taxes and the tax system? _____

_____

_____

_____

27. What kind of tax is the federal government's main source of income? _____

_____

_____

28. What kind of tax is the leading source of revenue for many state governments? _____

_____

29. What are excise taxes? Name six products that are subject to excise taxes. _____

_____

_____

_____

_____

_____

30. What are customs duties and tariffs? _____

_____

_____

31. Name the two principles that are used to ensure that taxes are applied fairly. _____

_____

_____

32. What is the key characteristic of a progressive tax? _____

_____

_____

33. Identify five major spending categories for state and local tax revenue. _____

_____

_____

_____

_____

Chapter 5 The U.S. Economic System

Social Services

Directions: One of the main goals of the U.S. economic system is security for its citizens. That includes support systems for people who face economic hardship through no fault of their own. Read the following hypothetical situations. Take on the role of a social worker and suggest a program or programs that might benefit the people described. Refer to pages 141-143 of the text.

1. Debbi Greenwood works as a home health aide for elderly residents of the community who have opted not to enter nursing homes. Debbi has health insurance through her job, but her children, a first grader and third grader, do not. She sends peanut butter and jelly sandwiches to school with them almost every day.

   _____
   _____
   _____
   _____
   _____

2. Mrs. Giftos had to quit work to care for her 8-month-old triplets. The girls were two months premature. Her husband is an assistant manager at a restaurant.

   _____
   _____
   _____

3. Carl Hancock, age 67, has a modest pension and supplemental health insurance through the construction company where he was employed for many years. What government program will send him a monthly check as a retirement benefit? If he should get sick, what related program would pay for the bulk of any hospitalization and medical expenses?

   _____
   _____
   _____
   _____

4. Tanya Rogers hopes to be working as a preschool teacher in two years. Now that her three children are in school, the single mother has gone back to college to earn her degree in early childhood education. Although Tanya receives a monthly child support check from her ex-husband, the family doesn't have enough money to buy food to last the entire month.

   _____
   _____
   _____
   _____

 **Activity**

Chapter 5 The U.S. Economic System

Types of Taxes

Directions: Abby and her mother, Rosa, work at the same nursing home 25 miles from home. Abby works nights in housekeeping and earns $6.50 per hour—about $13,500 per year. Her mother works during the day as the staff social worker, earning an annual salary of $40,000. Read the tax situations described below, then complete the items as directed.

1. To help determine the taxes that Abby and Rosa pay, calculate their weekly pay.

   a. How much does Abby earn per week if she works 40 hours? _$260_

   b. About how much does Rosa earn per week? _$1000_

2. Both women must spend about $35 per week on gasoline for commuting to work. Assume that gasoline tax accounts for 30% of the cost of the fuel.

   a. How much does each woman pay in gasoline taxes each week? Show how you arrived at that figure. _$37.45   Multiplied 35 by 7%. took the sum and added the 2 together_

   b. What percentage of Abby's income is spent on gasoline taxes? Show your calculation. _idk_

   c. What percentage of her mother's income is spent on the gasoline taxes? Show your calculation. _idk_

   d. Which type of tax does this situation demonstrate—proportional, progressive, or regressive? Why? _regressive_

3. Taxpayers in the state where Abby and Rosa live are required to pay a flat 3% state income tax. Assume that the tax applies to Abby and Rosa's entire income.

   a. How much is Abby's state income tax for the year? _$40.50_

   b. How much would Rosa pay? _$1,200_

   c. Which type of tax does this situation demonstrate? Why? _proportional_

4. Rosa pays more than 15% of her salary to the federal government for income tax. Her daughter pays much less. Which type of tax does this situation demonstrate? Explain.
   proportional

Name_____ Date _____ Class _____

Chapter 6 The Health of the Economy 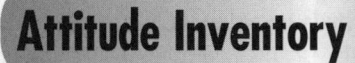 Attitude Inventory

Directions: Before you begin Chapter 6, take stock of your attitudes by completing the following inventory. Read each statement and check the appropriate column to indicate whether you agree, disagree, or are undecided. Use the space provided at the bottom of the page to write your comments about at least three of the statements. You will refer to this page again after completing your study of the chapter.

Statement	Agree	Disagree	Undecided
1. Economic slowdowns are to be expected from time to time.			
2. A healthy economy provides people with low prices and high wages.			
3. Inflation is a serious concern for consumers.			
4. Consumers who feel pessimistic about the nation's economic outlook can create a self-fulfilling prophecy.			
5. When a country goes to war, the economy tends to go into a decline.			
6. Statistics about the economy are of interest primarily to economists and politicians.			
7. Economic conditions in other countries generally don't affect U.S. consumers.			
8. Just as consumers should not spend money they don't have, neither should governments.			
9. Taxes should be raised in order to reduce the federal debt.			
10. The government should permanently set low interest rates for loans and high interest rates for savings accounts.			

Comments: _____

_____

_____

_____

_____

_____

_____

(Continued on next page)

Consumer Education & Economics Student Activity Manual
Copyright © Glencoe/McGraw-Hill

Name_____ Date_____ Class _____

Rechecking Your Attitude

Directions: After completing your study of Chapter 6, respond to the Attitude Inventory statements a second time. Then compare your two sets of responses. Use the space provided at the bottom of the page to note which of your answers changed. What do you think accounts for these shifts in your opinions? Explain in the space provided.

Statement	Agree	Disagree	Undecided
1. Economic slowdowns are to be expected from time to time.			
2. A healthy economy provides people with low prices and high wages.			
3. Inflation is a serious concern for consumers.			
4. Consumers who feel pessimistic about the nation's economic outlook can create a self-fulfilling prophecy.			
5. When a country goes to war, the economy tends to go into a decline.			
6. Statistics about the economy are of interest primarily to economists and politicians.			
7. Economic conditions in other countries generally don't affect U.S. consumers.			
8. Just as consumers should not spend money they don't have, neither should governments.			
9. Taxes should be raised in order to reduce the federal debt.			
10. The government should permanently set low interest rates for loans and high interest rates for savings accounts.			

Answers changed: _____

Why? _____

_____

_____

_____

_____

_____

Chapter 6 The Health of the Economy

Study Guide

Directions: As you read Chapter 6, answer the following questions. Later you can use this study guide to review chapter information.

Section 6.1 Economic Ups and Downs

1. What are the four phases of the business cycle? _____
   _____

2. Summarize what happens during a recession. _____
   _____
   _____
   _____
   _____

3. What is inflation? _____
   _____

4. Why is inflation particularly hard on people on fixed incomes? _____
   _____
   _____

5. Identify four factors that appear to trigger economic ups and downs. _____
   _____
   _____

6. How does consumer gloom about the future affect the economy? _____
   _____
   _____

7. Identify three economic indicators used to monitor the health of the economy. _____
   _____
   _____

8. What is the consumer price index based on? _____
   _____
   _____

Section 6.2 Deficits and Debt

9. What is the goal of the budget process? _____
   _____
   _____
   _____

(Continued on next page)

10. What is deficit spending? _____

_____

_____

11. How does buying a savings bond benefit both the buyer and the government? _____

_____

_____

_____

12. What is the term used for the amount of money the government owes? _____

_____

Section 6.3 Stabilizing the Economy

13. How does a government decision to cut personal taxes help the economy? _____

_____

_____

_____

_____

14. What is the primary responsibility of the Federal Reserve System? _____

_____

15. What happens when the Fed increases the money supply? _____

_____

_____

16. What happens when the Fed decreases the money supply? _____

_____

_____

_____

Name_____ Date_____ Class_____

Chapter 6 The Health of the Economy

Time Traveling Dollars

Directions: Imagine you're an inventor living in the year 1915. You've just invented a time machine! To test it, you decide to make a series of short hops, jumping forward five years in time with each trip. After you arrive in each year, you'll need to make a variety of purchases including food, clothing, housing, and other commonly used goods and services. How much will the items on your shopping list cost in each year you visit? Use the formula, tables, and example below to calculate the answers.

Formula

Current Year CPI ÷
Past Year CPI
× Past Year Price =
Price in Current Year

Year	CPI
1915	10.1
1920	20.0
1925	17.5
1930	16.7
1935	13.7
1940	14.0
1945	18.0
1950	24.1
1955	26.8

Year	CPI
1960	29.6
1965	31.5
1970	38.8
1975	53.8
1980	82.4
1985	107.6
1990	130.7
1995	152.4
2000	172.2

Example

In 1915, the items on your shopping list cost $200. You then travel forward in time to 1920. How much do the same items cost in 1920 dollars?

20.0 ÷ 10.1 × 200 = $396.04

Source: Federal Reserve Bank of Minneapolis

1. From 1920, you travel to 1925. How much do the items on your shopping list cost in 1925 dollars? Show your calculation. _17.5×20.0 = $350_

_____

Continue calculating the cost of your purchases in each year. Show your calculations.

2. 1930: $292.25

3. 1935: $228.79

4. 1940: $191.80

5. 1945: $252

6. 1950: $433.80

7. 1955: $645.88

8. 1960: $793.28

9. 1965: $932.40

10. 1970: $1,222.20

11. 1975: $2,087.44

12. 1980: $4,433.12

13. 1985: $8,866.24

14. 1990: $14,063.32

15. 1995: $19,918.68

16. 2000: $26,243.28

 **Activity**

Chapter 6 The Health of the Economy

Your Federal Budget

Directions: The federal government spends billions of dollars each year on dozens of different programs. Fifteen such programs or possibilities are listed below in alphabetical order. Study them, then answer the questions that follow.

_____ Aid to people with disabilities

_____ Conservation and wildlife preservation

_____ Consumer protection

_____ Development of alternative energy sources

_____ Economic aid to cities

_____ Educational loans (individuals) and grants (school systems)

_____ Funding for libraries and museums

_____ Government jobs for the unemployed

_____ Guaranteed national income

_____ Mass transit

_____ National defense

_____ Health insurance for the elderly

_____ Social Security payment increases for retired people

_____ Subsidies to businesses

_____ Welfare payment increases

1. Assume that you have the power to determine federal spending priorities. Which program would you rank first? Second? Continue numbering the items through fifteen.

2. Check the accuracy of your list. Assume you have to reduce spending by one-third. Rather than cut across the board, you decide to eliminate funding for five programs.

   a. Which five? _____

   _____

   _____

   b. Where did these programs fall in your rankings? _____

   c. If any of the programs you choose to eliminate fell in the first half of your list, go back and reanalyze your priorities. Then renumber.

3. Assume that to reduce the federal deficit, you have to cut spending by yet another third. You can either eliminate three more programs or reduce funding for all ten by the same amount. Which would you do and why? If you choose to eliminate programs, specify which ones.

_____

_____

_____

_____

_____

_____

Chapter 7 Global Economics

Directions: Before you begin Chapter 7, take stock of your attitudes by completing the following inventory. Read each statement and check the appropriate column to indicate whether you agree, disagree, or are undecided. Use the space provided at the bottom of the page to write your comments about at least three of the statements. You will refer to this page again after completing your study of the chapter.

Statement	Agree	Disagree	Undecided
1. It's to a nation's advantage to be self-sufficient rather than trading with other nations.			
2. World trade promotes world peace.			
3. When U.S. businesses face foreign competition, consumers can benefit.			
4. The government should restrict imports in order to protect American jobs.			
5. It would be desirable to have one worldwide currency.			
6. In recent years, the U.S. has been selling more to other countries than it purchases from them.			
7. Foreign ownership of companies in the U.S. is a matter of concern.			
8. Dependence on foreign oil threatens national security.			
9. On the whole, it's best to minimize trade restrictions.			
10. People in other countries should strive to maintain their own cultures rather than becoming "Americanized."			

Comments: _____

_____

_____

_____

_____

_____

_____

(Continued on next page)

Name_____ Date_____ Class _____

Rechecking Your Attitude

Directions: After completing your study of Chapter 7, respond to the Attitude Inventory statements a second time. Then compare your two sets of responses. Use the space provided at the bottom of the page to note which of your answers changed. What do you think accounts for these shifts in your opinions? Explain in the space provided.

Statement	Agree	Disagree	Undecided
1. It's to a nation's advantage to be self-sufficient rather than trading with other nations.			
2. World trade promotes world peace.			
3. When U.S. businesses face foreign competition, consumers can benefit.			
4. The government should restrict imports in order to protect American jobs.			
5. It would be desirable to have one worldwide currency.			
6. In recent years, the U.S. has been selling more to other countries than it purchases from them.			
7. Foreign ownership of companies in the U.S. is a matter of concern.			
8. Dependence on foreign oil threatens national security.			
9. On the whole, it's best to minimize trade restrictions.			
10. People in other countries should strive to maintain their own cultures rather than becoming "Americanized."			

Answers changed: _____

Why? _____

_____

_____

_____

_____

_____

Consumer Education & Economics Student Activity Manual
Copyright © Glencoe/McGraw-Hill

Chapter 7 Global Economics

Directions: As you read Chapter 7, answer the following questions. Later you can use this study guide to review chapter information.

Section 7.1 Trade Between Nations

1. What are imports? Identify five categories of imports. _____
_____
_____
_____

2. According to Adam Smith, how could a nation increase its productivity and wealth?
_____
_____
_____

3. What is the advantage of having every nation specialize in the goods it produces most efficiently? _____
_____
_____

4. In what ways does international trade benefit consumers? _____
_____
_____
_____

5. How does international trade contribute to prosperity? _____
_____
_____

6. Why do flexible exchange rates make the cost of doing business unpredictable? _____
_____
_____
_____

7. What do many countries do to control the value of their currency? _____
_____
_____
_____

(Continued on next page)

Study Guide *(Continued)*

8. How does the strength of the U.S. dollar affect the nation's exports? _____
_____
_____

9. What happens when a country spends more on imports than it receives for exports?
_____
_____
_____

10. Identify the two main types of transactions that are recorded in a country's balance of payments.
_____
_____
_____

Section 7.2 Trade Restrictions and Agreements

11. What are the three main methods of restricting trade? _____
_____

12. What is the difference between protectionism and free trade? _____
_____
_____
_____
_____

13. How does protectionism help infant industries? _____
_____
_____

14. Why does free trade promote competition? _____
_____
_____
_____

15. What was the goal of the General Agreement on Tariffs and Trade (GATT)? _____
_____
_____

16. What is the North American Free Trade Agreement (NAFTA)?_____
_____
_____

Consumer Education & Economics Student Activity Manual
Copyright © Glencoe/McGraw-Hill

Chapter 7 Global Economics

Activity

Around the World

Directions: Imagine that you're going on a trip around the world. As you arrive in each new country or region, you must exchange the currency you're carrying for local currency. Calculate each currency conversion using the information provided. Show your calculations.

1. You begin your journey by traveling to Chile. On the day you arrive, the exchange rate is 695 Chilean pesos for every U.S. dollar. You have 500 U.S. dollars to exchange. How many Chilean pesos are they worth?

    $347,500 Pesos

2. When you leave Chile, you have 295,800 pesos to exchange. Your next stop is Morocco. The exchange rate is 0.015 Moroccan dirhams for every Chilean peso. How many dirhams are your Chilean pesos worth?

    $4437 dirhams

3. After spending several days in Morocco, you prepare for your next stop—Italy. The Italians use the common European currency, the euro. The exchange rate that day is 0.09 euros for every Moroccan dirham. How many euros are equal to the 3,600 dirhams that you have left?

    £324

4. Next, you travel to Russia. You have 248 euros in your pocket when you visit the bank to exchange your currency. The bank teller says today's exchange rate is 31 Russian rubles for every euro. How many Russian rubles are your euros worth?

    Rubles 7,804

5. From Russia, your journey takes you to China. In exchange for every Russian ruble, you can receive 0.25 of the Chinese currency called yuan renminbi. You have 5,324 rubles to exchange. How many yuan renminbi are they worth?

    1,331 renminbi

6. Your next stop is the land down under—Australia. The currency in Australia is called the dollar, but it's not the same as the U.S. dollar. The exchange rate is 0.22 Australian dollars for every Chinese yuan renminbi. You have 700 yuan to exchange. How many Australian dollars are they worth?

    154 dollars

7. Your world tour is almost over—it's time to come home. You're left with 75 Australian dollars to exchange. At a rate of 0.56 U.S. dollars for one Australian dollar, how many U.S. dollars do you have at the end of your journey?

    $42

(Continued on next page)

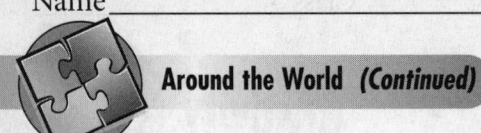

8. The table below shows the value of a number of currencies compared to the U.S. dollar on a hypothetical day. Use that information to calculate the following conversions. Show your calculations.

Exchange rates for one U.S. dollar (on a hypothetical day)	
2.81 Brazilian reals	119.72 Japanese yen
0.65 British pounds	9.96 Mexican pesos
1.52 Canadian dollars	2.06 New Zealand dollars
4.66 Egyptian pounds	2,606.90 Somalian shillings
48.88 Indian rupees	9.19 Swedish kronor

HINT: To convert one of the listed currencies to U.S. dollars, divide by the exchange rate shown. For example, 13 British pounds ÷ 0.65 = 20 U.S. dollars. Then convert U.S. dollars to the other currency.

a. 13 British pounds = how many Egyptian pounds?

_____

_____

_____

b. 130,345 Somalian shillings = how many Brazilian reals?

_____

_____

_____

c. 1,992 Mexican pesos = how many Swedish kronor?

_____

_____

_____

d. 76 Canadian dollars = how many New Zealand dollars?

_____

_____

_____

e. 718,320 Japanese yen = how many Indian rupees?

_____

_____

_____

Name_____ Date_____ Class_____

Chapter 8 Income and Taxes

Directions: Before you begin Chapter 8, take stock of your attitudes by completing the following inventory. Read each statement and check the appropriate column to indicate whether you agree, disagree, or are undecided. Use the space provided at the bottom of the page to write your comments about at least three of the statements. You will refer to this page again after completing your study of the chapter.

Statement	Agree	Disagree	Undecided
1. Being paid a set yearly salary is preferable to being paid by the hour.			
2. In any given job, employees who have families to support should receive higher pay than employees who are single.			
3. The government could increase prosperity by raising the minimum wage.			
4. When choosing between two job offers, the one that pays more is always better from a financial standpoint.			
5. All employees should be paid extra for working overtime.			
6. Workers who expect to be paid tips are cheating consumers by making them pay twice.			
7. Hiring temporary workers instead of adding permanent staff positions is not a good solution for businesses in the long run.			
8. If you are hired to work for $500 per week, that's how much you will receive.			
9. Paying federal income tax is voluntary.			
10. Taxpayers should take full advantage of any income tax breaks to which they are entitled.			

Comments: _____

_____

_____

_____

_____

_____

(Continued on next page)

Consumer Education & Economics Student Activity Manual
Copyright © Glencoe/McGraw-Hill

Name_____ Date_____ Class _____

Rechecking Your Attitude

Directions: After completing your study of Chapter 8, respond to the Attitude Inventory statements a second time. Then compare your two sets of responses. Use the space provided at the bottom of the page to note which of your answers changed. What do you think accounts for these shifts in your opinions? Explain in the space provided.

Statement	Agree	Disagree	Undecided
1. Being paid a set yearly salary is preferable to being paid by the hour.			
2. In any given job, employees who have families to support should receive higher pay than employees who are single.			
3. The government could increase prosperity by raising the minimum wage.			
4. When choosing between two job offers, the one that pays more is always better from a financial standpoint.			
5. All employees should be paid extra for working overtime.			
6. Workers who expect to be paid tips are cheating consumers by making them pay twice.			
7. Hiring temporary workers instead of adding permanent staff positions is not a good solution for businesses in the long run.			
8. If you are hired to work for $500 per week, that's how much you will receive.			
9. Paying federal income tax is voluntary.			
10. Taxpayers should take full advantage of any income tax breaks to which they are entitled.			

Answers changed: _____

Why? _____

_____

_____

_____

_____

_____

Chapter 8 Income and Taxes

Directions: As you read Chapter 8, answer the following questions. Later you can use this study guide to review chapter information.

Section 8.1 Examining Pay and Benefits

1. Explain the difference between a bonus and tips. _____
   _____
   _____
   _____

2. What is the purpose of the equal pay provisions of the Fair Labor Standards Act? _____
   _____
   _____

3. Why do you need to consider benefits as well as pay when evaluating different jobs?_____
   _____
   _____
   _____

4. What is the difference between part-time work and temporary work? _____
   _____
   _____
   _____

5. What are the advantages to employers of using temporary and contract workers? _____
   _____
   _____
   _____
   _____
   _____

Section 8.2 Understanding Your Paycheck

6. If you are paid by direct deposit, how is your payment made? _____
   _____
   _____
   _____

7. What information appears on a pay stub? _____
   _____
   _____

(Continued on next page)

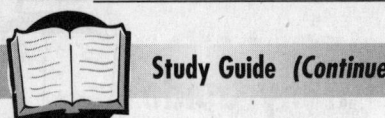

8. What do your deductions for Social Security and Medicare pay for? _____

_____

_____

_____

9. Which is the smaller amount on a pay stub—gross pay or net pay? Why is it smaller? _____

_____

_____

_____

_____

_____

Section 8.3 Paying Income Taxes

10. How is the amount of income tax you pay determined? _____

_____

_____

11. What is the purpose of a tax return? _____

_____

_____

12. What information appears on a Form W-2? _____

_____

_____

13. What does the tax table in the IRS instruction booklet tell you? _____

_____

_____

14. When do people qualify for a tax refund? _____

_____

15. Why is it a good idea to review your W-4 allowances periodically? _____

_____

_____

_____

Consumer Education & Economics Student Activity Manual
Copyright © Glencoe/McGraw-Hill

Name_____ Date_____ Class _____

Chapter 8 Income and Taxes

Paycheck Deductions

Directions: Read the following descriptions of two employment situations—one for a part-time wage earner, the other for a full-time salaried employee. Compute the employees' pay and deductions to fill in their paycheck stubs.

1. Hannah, a college student majoring in journalism, is working as a copy messenger at the local daily newspaper. She works 20 hours per week for a wage of $10.50 per hour. Although she works part time, she is responsible for paying union dues. Employees at the newspaper are paid weekly.

   The following deductions are taken out of Hannah's paycheck each week:

   • Union dues: 2% of gross pay

   • Federal income tax (FED TX): 10% of gross pay

   • State income tax (ST TX): 3% of gross pay

   • Social Security tax (SOC SEC): 6.2% of gross pay

   • Medicare tax (MEDI): 1.45% of gross pay

   Use the information above to fill out Hannah's paycheck stub, rounding to the nearest cent:

GROSS PAY	$10902
FED TX	$1090.20
MEDI	$158.08
SOC SEC	$675.92
ST TX	$327.06
UNION	$218.04
TOTAL DED	$2469.30
NET PAY	$ 8,432.7

2. Eli is working in marketing for a national corporation. He earns a salary of $35,000 and is paid every two weeks (26 times a year).

   The following deductions are taken out of Eli's biweekly paycheck:

   • Federal income tax (FED TX): 10% of gross pay

   • State income tax (ST TX): 3.5% of gross pay

   • Social Security tax (SOC SEC): 6.2% of gross pay

   • Medicare tax (MEDI): 1.45% of gross pay

(Continued on next page)

Use the information on the previous page to fill out Eli's biweekly paycheck stub, rounding to the nearest cent:

GROSS PAY	$35000
FED TX	$3,500
MEDI	$507.50
SOC SEC	$2170
ST TX	$1225
TOTAL DED	$7402.50
NET PAY	$27,507.50

3. Eli learns that he is getting a 4% raise. What is his new annual salary? $36400

Revise Eli's biweekly paycheck stub to reflect his raise, rounding to the nearest cent:

GROSS PAY	$35000
FED TX	$3500
MEDI	$508
SOC SEC	$2170
ST TX	$1225
TOTAL DED	$7403
NET PAY	$27,598

Chapter 8 Income and Taxes

Tax Time

Directions: Filling out a tax return correctly requires attention to detail, the ability to follow instructions exactly, and good math skills. Use the information provided below, along with the textbook chapter, to complete the items as directed.

Joe is unmarried, lives alone, and does not support anyone financially. He has savings and checking accounts at a credit union and another savings account at a bank. Last year he lost his job in April and was unemployed for about three months. He found another job after taking community college classes to enhance his skills.

Joe is getting ready to file his federal tax return. The first thing he does is gather the forms he will need.

1. What form, sent to Joe by each of his employers, shows the amount of income he earned and how much income tax was withheld? _W-4_____

2. What form, sent to Joe by his bank and his credit union, shows how much interest income he earned? _W-2_____

The forms show that Joe's old employer paid him $9,720.34 in taxable income and withheld $1,354.76 for federal income tax. At his new job, Joe earned $23,105.58 in taxable income and had $3,425.36 federal income tax withheld. Joe earned $232.47 in taxable interest from his credit union and $186.12 from his bank. He received $4,238.00 in unemployment compensation.

Joe also prints out his spending records showing where his money went last year. He made a tax-deductible contribution to his IRA (individual retirement account) in the amount of $500. He calculates that his tax-deductible expenses for the past year total $2,387.44.

Next, Joe must decide which form to use for filing his return. When he checks the instructions, he learns the following:

- Only single people with no dependents may use Form 1040EZ.
- The standard deduction this year is $4,550 for single taxpayers.
- Persons with more than $400 in interest income cannot use Form 1040EZ.
- Taxpayers who wish to itemize deductions cannot use Form 1040EZ or 1040A.
- Any taxpayer may use Form 1040.

3. Which tax form is probably the best choice for Joe's situation? Why? _1st option_
   He's single, and nobody depends on him for money.
   _____
   _____
   _____
   _____
   _____

(Continued on next page)

For his filing status, Joe checks the "Single" box. Next, he must calculate and enter the number of exemptions he is claiming.

4. How many exemptions can Joe claim? Why? <u>One, there is only 1 tax exemption</u>
   <u>per household</u>
   _____

Joe begins filling out the return to calculate the tax he owes. Fill in the blanks below to show what information he should enter on the return.

5. Wages, salaries, tips, etc. . . . . 5. $ <u>23,105.58</u>

6. Taxable interest . . . . 6. $ _____

7. Unemployment compensation . . . . 7. $ _____

8. Add lines 5, 6, and 7. This is Joe's total income. . . . . 8. $ _____

9. Deduction for IRA contribution . . . . 9. $ _____

10. Subtract line 9 from line 8. This is Joe's adjusted gross income. . . . . 10. $ _____

11. Enter the amount of Joe's itemized deductions OR the standard
    deduction, whichever will cause him to pay less tax. . . . . 11. $ _____

12. Subtract line 11 from line 10. . . . . 12. $ _____

13. Multiply $2,900 by the total number of exemptions (see item 4). . . . . . 13. $ _____

14. Subtract line 13 from line 12. This is Joe's taxable income. . . . . 14. $ _____

15. Use the tax table below to find the amount of Joe's tax based on
    his taxable income. . . . . 15. $ _____

16. Joe is eligible for an education credit based on the tuition he
    paid for college classes. He uses a worksheet to calculate the
    credit. Multiply $450 (the amount of Joe's tuition) by 20% (.20). . . . . . . 16. $ _____

17. Subtract line 16 from line 15. This is Joe's total tax. . . . . 17. $ _____

18. Enter the total amount of tax that was withheld from Joe's
    pay during the year. . . . . 18. $ _____

19. Is Joe getting a tax refund, or does he need to make a payment to the IRS?
    Specify the amount of the refund or payment. _____

Tax Table

Taxable Income		And you are—			
At least	But less than	Single	Married filing jointly *	Married filing separately	Head of a house-hold
					Your tax is—
29,000					
29,000	29,050	4,601	4,354	5,157	4,354
29,050	29,100	4,614	4,361	5,171	4,361
29,100	29,150	4,628	4,369	5,184	4,369
29,150	29,200	4,642	4,376	5,198	4,376
29,200	29,250	4,656	4,384	5,212	4,384

29,150					1,376
29,200	29,250	4,656	4,384	5,212	4,384
29,250	29,300	4,669	4,391	5,226	4,391
29,300	29,350	4,683	4,399	5,239	4,399
29,350	29,400	4,697	4,406	5,253	4,406
29,400	29,450	4,711	4,414	5,267	4,414
29,450	29,500	4,724	4,421	5,281	4,421
29,500	29,550	4,738	4,429	5,294	4,429
29,550	29,600	4,752	4,436	5,308	4,436
29,600	29,650	4,766	4,444	5,322	4,444
29,650	29,700	4,779	4,451	5,336	4,451
29,700	29,750	4,793	4,459	5,349	4,459
29,750	29,800	4,807	4,466	5,363	4,466
29,800	29,850	4,821	4,474	5,377	4,474
29,850	29,900	4,834	4,481	5,391	4,481
29,900	29,950	4,848	4,489	5,404	4,489
29,950	30,000	4,862	4,496	5,418	4,496

Name_____ Date_____ Class_____

Chapter 9 Financial Planning

Directions: Before you begin Chapter 9, take stock of your attitudes by completing the following inventory. Read each statement and check the appropriate column to indicate whether you agree, disagree, or are undecided. Use the space provided at the bottom of the page to write your comments about at least three of the statements. You will refer to this page again after completing your study of the chapter.

Statement	Agree	Disagree	Undecided
1. People who are easily able to live within their income do not need a financial plan.			
2. When I begin living on my own, I expect to live as well as or better than I do now.			
3. A financial plan should change to fit changing circumstances.			
4. Paying bills on the Internet is preferable to paying them by sending checks through the mail.			
5. If you can keep track of spending in your head, there is no need to keep a budget or expense record.			
6. Someone who has an uncertain or variable income will find a budget especially useful.			
7. The family budget should be the sole responsibility of one person.			
8. Once a budget has been drawn up, it should not be changed.			
9. It's best to keep all financial records for as long as possible.			
10. It's better to handle your finances yourself than to trust them to anyone else.			

Comments: _____

_____

_____

_____

_____

_____

_____

(Continued on next page)

Rechecking Your Attitude

Directions: After completing your study of Chapter 9, respond to the Attitude Inventory statements a second time. Then compare your two sets of responses. Use the space provided at the bottom of the page to note which of your answers changed. What do you think accounts for these shifts in your opinions? Explain in the space provided.

Statement	Agree	Disagree	Undecided
1. People who are easily able to live within their income do not need a financial plan.			
2. When I begin living on my own, I expect to live as well as or better than I do now.			
3. A financial plan should change to fit changing circumstances.			
4. Paying bills on the Internet is preferable to paying them by sending checks through the mail.			
5. If you can keep track of spending in your head, there is no need to keep a budget or expense record.			
6. Someone who has an uncertain or variable income will find a budget especially useful.			
7. The family budget should be the sole responsibility of one person.			
8. Once a budget has been drawn up, it should not be changed.			
9. It's best to keep all financial records for as long as possible.			
10. It's better to handle your finances yourself than to trust them to anyone else.			

Answers changed: _____

Why? _____

_____

_____

_____

_____

Chapter 9 Financial Planning

Study Guide

Directions: As you read Chapter 9, answer the following questions. Later you can use this study guide to review chapter information.

Section 9.1 Looking at Your Finances

1. What does living within your means involve? _____
_____
_____
_____

2. Why do you need to define your financial goals? _____
_____
_____
_____

3. How do you determine your net worth? _____
_____
_____

4. Why is it a good idea to analyze your spending habits? _____
_____
_____

5. Why do family members need to review and revise their financial plans as they go through different life stages? _____
_____
_____
_____
_____
_____

Section 9.2 Using Financial Software

6. What does the checkbook feature of financial software enable you to do? _____
_____
_____
_____
_____

(Continued on next page)

7. How does financial software help you with budgeting? _____

_____

_____

8. What do online bill payment and online bill presentment involve? _____

_____

_____

9. Identify two advantages of paying bills online. _____

_____

_____

10. What research can you do to learn about available financial software packages? _____

_____

_____

_____

_____

11. If you need help when using financial software, how can you get it? _____

_____

_____

_____

12. Why is it a good idea to stay aware of upgrades on any software you buy? _____

_____

_____

Section 9.3 Creating a Budget

13. What is a budget? _____

_____

_____

14. Identify the three main tasks involved in budgeting. _____

_____

_____

15. What is the difference between fixed expenses and variable expenses? _____

_____

_____

_____

16. What documents can help you analyze your past spending? _____
_____
_____

17. Why is it a good idea to treat savings just like any other expense category? _____
_____
_____
_____

18. Which kind of expenses are often the easiest to cut? _____
_____
_____

19. Identify four ways a person can increase income in order to balance a budget. _____
_____
_____
_____

20. What do you need to do if you consistently spend more than you budgeted in a particular budget category? _____
_____

21. Why does an effective budget need to be flexible? _____
_____
_____

Section 9.4 Organizing Your Records

22. Identify two advantages of setting up a system for storing records and documents.
_____
_____
_____

23. Why is it a good idea to keep cancelled checks? _____
_____

24. Why do you need to keep records of financial transactions? _____
_____
_____
_____

(Continued on next page)

25. What kinds of documents might be stored in a safe deposit box? _____

_____

_____

26. What kinds of records would you keep in a home filing system? _____

_____

27. How often should you review your records? What should you do with old records? _____

_____

_____

Section 9.5 Seeking Professional Advice

28. If you need help managing your finances, what might you do instead of consulting a
professional? _____

_____

29. What does the Certified Financial Planner designation indicate? _____

_____

_____

_____

30. For what financial services might you need an attorney? _____

_____

_____

_____

31. What should consumers be concerned about if they hire a financial professional who earns a
commission on the products he or she sells? _____

_____

_____

32. Why is it a good idea to ask a financial adviser to provide references from clients? _____

_____

_____

_____

_____

Chapter 9 Financial Planning

Handwritten: 475 / +485 / 960

Budget Basics

Directions: Josh has decided to create and follow a budget. Use the information below to complete the items as directed.

Josh takes home $1,155 a month. He has the following estimated expenses for March.

Car payment.........................$150
Church donations $20
Dad's birthday $30
Dry cleaning.........................$20
Entertainment.......................$100
Gas (car) $75

Gas and electricity
  (apt.)...............................$25
Glasses (new
  prescription) $150
Groceries $100
Meals out $100

Rent $200
Savings (50% of savings to
  emergency fund) $150
Subscriptions......................$10
Telephone..........................$25

1. Complete Josh's budget plan based on his estimated expenses.

Handwritten: 1160 / +225 / 1385   150

SAVINGS		
Emergency fund	75	$ 75
Savings account	75	$ 150
FIXED EXPENSES		
Rent	200	$ 200
Installment loan(s)	150	$
Other		$
FLEXIBLE EXPENSES		
Food	200	$ 200
Utilities	50	$ 225
Household supplies and furnishings		$ 45
Clothing		$
Auto: gas and maintenance		$ 150
Misc. health care products and services		$ 150
Entertainment		$ 100
Personal		$ 35
Gifts and contributions		$ 50

Left margin handwritten: 75, 75, 200, 150, 200, 50, 75, 100, 100, 20, 50

Total savings: 150 $ 225

Total fixed expenses: 350 $ 200

Handwritten: 960
Total flexible expenses: 665 $ ~~45~~
1385
Total savings & expenses: 1155 $ ~~160~~

Total income: 1155 – 1155 / 230 $ 1385
Handwritten: 1385

Difference: $ –230

2. What percentage of his take-home pay is Josh spending on each of the following items? Show your calculations.

a. Food: _____ $300 _ 17.32% _____

b. Housing (rent and utilities): ___ $425 _ 21.65% ____

c. Transportation: _____ $150 _ 6.49% _____

(Continued on next page)

d. Medical expenses: _$150 13.85%_

e. Savings: _$225 12.99%_

f. Entertainment: _$100 8.66%_

3. Because of a shortage of parts, the plant where Josh works will be shut down for five days in April. As a result, Josh's monthly take-home pay will be reduced to $860. Josh isn't sure how he will make ends meet. Using March's expenses as a starting point, plan a second budget for Josh and show him how he can manage.

SAVINGS	
Emergency fund	$ 55.86
Savings account	$ 55.86
FIXED EXPENSES	
Rent	$ 139.65
Installment loan(s)	$
Other	$
FLEXIBLE EXPENSES	
Food	$ 148.95
Utilities	$ 46.55
Household supplies and furnishings	$
Clothing	$
Auto: gas and maintenance	$ 55.81
Misc. health care products and services	$ 119.11
Entertainment	$ 74.476
Personal	$
Gifts and contributions	$

Total savings: $ _____

Total fixed expenses: $ _____

Total flexible expenses: $ _____

Total savings & expenses: $ _____

Total income: $ _____

Difference: $ _____

4. In which categories did you make cuts? Why? _I dropped every category by Roughly 25%._

_____

_____

5. For each category you listed in question 4, give Josh at least one specific hint for holding down his expenses.

Cut off the unneeded expenses (eating out for things)

_____

_____

_____

_____

Chapter 10 Banking

Directions: Before you begin Chapter 10, take stock of your attitudes by completing the following inventory. Read each statement and check the appropriate column to indicate whether you agree, disagree, or are undecided. Use the space provided at the bottom of the page to write your comments about at least three of the statements. You will refer to this page again after completing your study of the chapter.

Statement	Agree	Disagree	Undecided
1. You can save money by shopping around for a financial institution.			
2. You can take your money out of the bank anytime you wish—after all, it's your money!			
3. Money that you deposit in a bank is stored in a vault until you withdraw it.			
4. A bank, a savings and loan, and a credit union are essentially the same thing.			
5. An ATM card makes it too easy to spend money.			
6. Electronic banking will eventually eliminate the need to use a teller window.			
7. Having a check canceled reflects badly on the person who wrote it.			
8. Reconciling a checking account is necessary only if you suspect a bank error.			
9. Anyone going on a long trip should take traveler's checks.			
10. Prepaid cards and other electronic payment methods will eventually replace cash.			

Comments: _____
_____
_____
_____
_____
_____
_____
_____

(Continued on next page)

 **Attitude Inventory (Continued)**

Rechecking Your Attitude

Directions: After completing your study of Chapter 10, respond to the Attitude Inventory statements a second time. Then compare your two sets of responses. Use the space provided at the bottom of the page to note which of your answers changed. What do you think accounts for these shifts in your opinions? Explain in the space provided.

Statement	Agree	Disagree	Undecided
1. You can save money by shopping around for a financial institution.			
2. You can take your money out of the bank anytime you wish—after all, it's your money!			
3. Money that you deposit in a bank is stored in a vault until you withdraw it.			
4. A bank, a savings and loan, and a credit union are essentially the same thing.			
5. An ATM card makes it too easy to spend money.			
6. Electronic banking will eventually eliminate the need to use a teller window.			
7. Having a check canceled reflects badly on the person who wrote it.			
8. Reconciling a checking account is necessary only if you suspect a bank error.			
9. Anyone going on a long trip should take traveler's checks.			
10. Prepaid cards and other electronic payment methods will eventually replace cash.			

Answers changed: _____

Why? _____

_____

_____

_____

_____

_____

Consumer Education & Economics Student Activity Manual
Copyright © Glencoe/McGraw-Hill

Name _____ Date _____ Class _____

Chapter 10 Banking

Directions: As you read Chapter 10, answer the following questions. Later you can use this study guide to review chapter information.

Section 10.1 Comparing Financial Institutions

1. What does a bank do with the money you deposit there? _____
   _____
   _____
   _____

2. What kinds of bank customers pay the bank interest? What kinds receive interest from the bank?
   _____
   _____
   _____

3. Describe the advantages that Internet banks have over traditional banks. _____
   _____
   _____
   _____
   _____
   _____
   _____

4. How does FDIC insurance protect you? _____
   _____
   _____
   _____

5. What factors do you need to consider when choosing a financial institution? _____
   _____
   _____
   _____

Section 10.2 Banking Electronically

6. Identify the four most common uses of ATMs. _____
   _____
   _____
   _____

(Continued on next page)

7. What do you need to understand before you use an ATM card? _____

_____

_____

_____

8. What is a debit card? _____

_____

_____

_____

9. Summarize the advantages and disadvantages of using a debit card instead of writing a check.

_____

_____

_____

_____

_____

_____

10. Identify three typical banking activities that you can do by telephone. _____

_____

_____

_____

_____

11. List three advantages of using online banking. _____

_____

_____

_____

_____

_____

12. Why should you report the loss of an ATM or debit card within two days of the loss? _____

_____

_____

_____

_____

_____

Section 10.3 Managing a Checking Account

13. Give two advantages that checks have over cash. _____

_____

_____

14. List the items to check out when comparing different checking accounts. _____

_____

_____

_____

_____

15. What information do you need to provide on a deposit slip? _____

_____

_____

16. What is an endorsement on a check? Why is it needed? _____

_____

_____

_____

_____

_____

17. What should you do if you make a mistake when writing a check? _____

_____

_____

_____

_____

18. What does reconciling a bank account involve? _____

_____

_____

_____

(Continued on next page)

Section 10.4 Using Other Payment Methods

19. What is a cashier's check? For what kinds of transactions might a cashier's check be required?

_____

_____

_____

_____

_____

_____

20. What advantage do traveler's checks have over cash? _____

_____

_____

_____

_____

21. Explain the difference between a money transfer and a wire transfer. _____

_____

_____

_____

_____

_____

_____

22. How do you use a prepaid card? _____

_____

_____

_____

_____

23. How do online payment services protect your security? _____

_____

_____

_____

_____

_____

Chapter 10 Banking

Activity

Deposit Slip

Directions: On your weekly visit to the bank, you have several deposits to make. Use the information below to fill out the deposit slip.

You want to deposit the following items in checking account number 603-130804:

- Your paycheck: $314.67
- A birthday gift from your grandparents: $50 bill
- A refund check from a local store: $29.12
- A personal check from a friend who owed you money: $20
- A rebate check from an out-of-state manufacturer: $1

You would like to receive $25 back in cash.

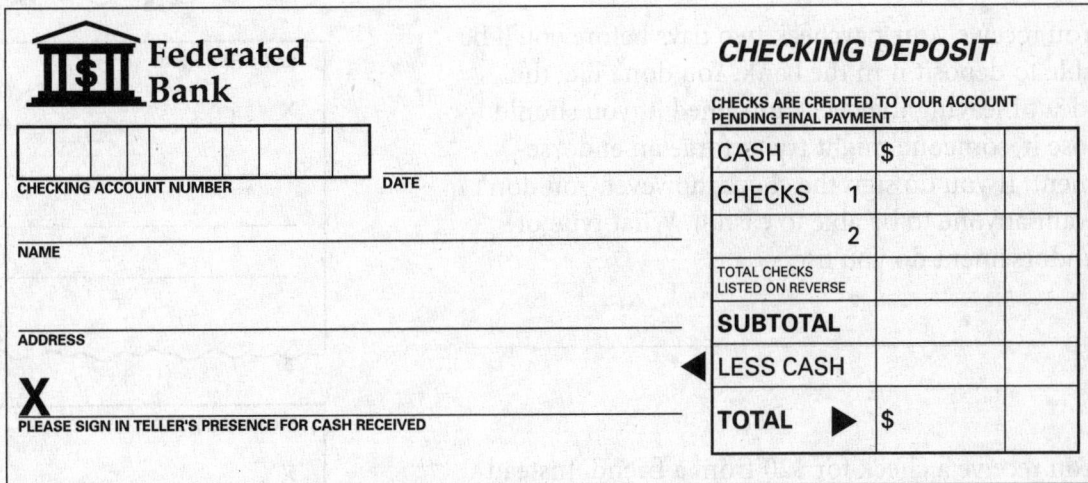

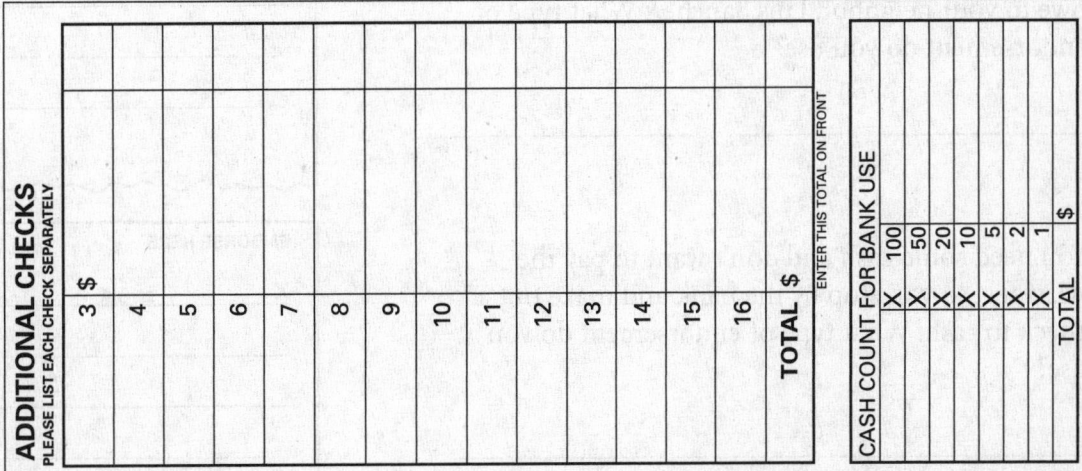

Activity

Endorsing Checks

Directions: There are several ways to endorse a check. Read the items below and decide what type of endorsement is called for in each situation. Endorse the check accordingly.

1. You're standing at the teller's window in the bank. The teller gives you a pen so that you can endorse the check you want to deposit. What type of endorsement do you use?

   _____

   ```
   ENDORSE HERE
   X _____
   _____
   _____
   ```

2. You receive your paycheck two days before you'll be able to deposit it in the bank. You don't like the idea of leaving the check unsigned; if you should lose it, someone might try to forge an endorsement. If you do sign the check, however, you don't want anyone to be able to cash it. What type of endorsement do you use?

   _____

   ```
   ENDORSE HERE
   X _____
   _____
   _____
   _____
   ```

3. You receive a check for $20 from a friend. Instead of depositing it, you use it to pay back the $20 you owe to your neighbor, Luis Sanchez. What type of endorsement do you use?

   _____

   ```
   ENDORSE HERE
   X _____
   _____
   _____
   _____
   ```

4. You need some cash and don't want to pay the ATM fee, so you stop by the bank and make out a check to cash. What type of endorsement do you use?

   _____

   ```
   ENDORSE HERE
   X _____
   _____
   _____
   _____
   ```

Consumer Education & Economics Student Activity Manual
Copyright © Glencoe/McGraw-Hill

Chapter 10 Banking

Activity

Writing Checks

Directions: Enter each of the following transactions in the check register below. For check transactions, fill out the blank checks on this and the following page and sign with your own name. The account number is 603-130804, and the beginning balance is $416.68. The last check you filled out was number 233.

March 7:   You buy a pair of shoes at Robinson's Department Store for $47.93.
March 12: You pay the premium ($350) on your automobile insurance policy. You are insured by Acme Insurance.
March 16: You deposit your paycheck ($314.67) in your checking account.
March 20: You pick up a prescription refill ($4) at Webster's Pharmacy and pay for it by check.
March 23: You mail a check to the Department of Water and Power to cover your electric bill ($55.06).

		RECORD ALL CHARGES OR CREDITS THAT AFFECT YOUR ACCOUNT					
NUMBER	DATE	DESCRIPTION OF TRANSACTION	PAYMENT/ DEBIT (–)	✓ T	FEE (IF ANY) (–)	DEPOSIT/ CREDIT (+)	BALANCE $

NAME _____   NO. ____
ACCOUNT NO. _____ _____ 2 ____

Pay to the order of _____ $ _____

_____ dollars

Federated Bank

for _____   _____

⑆122000247⑆   603130804⑈33

(Continued on next page)

Writing Checks *(Continued)*

NAME _____ NO. _____
ACCOUNT NO. _____ 2 _____

Pay to the
order of _____ $ _____

_____ dollars

Federated Bank

for _____ _____

⑆122000247⑆ 603130804⑈33

NAME _____ NO. _____
ACCOUNT NO. _____ 2 _____

Pay to the
order of _____ $ _____

_____ dollars

Federated Bank

for _____ _____

⑆122000247⑆ 603130804⑈33

NAME _____ NO. _____
ACCOUNT NO. _____ 2 _____

Pay to the
order of _____ $ _____

_____ dollars

Federated Bank

for _____ _____

⑆122000247⑆ 603130804⑈33

Name_____ Date_____ Class_____

Chapter 11 Consumer Credit

Directions: Before you begin Chapter 11, take stock of your attitudes by completing the following inventory. Read each statement and check the appropriate column to indicate whether you agree, disagree, or are undecided. Use the space provided at the bottom of the page to write your comments about at least three of the statements. You will refer to this page again after completing your study of the chapter.

Statement	Agree	Disagree	Undecided
1. Credit is far more important to older people than to young people and young families.			
2. Credit is easy to get if you don't need it.			
3. A good credit rating is not important to a consumer who always pays cash.			
4. A person can never have too many credit cards.			
5. The cost of credit is so small that it may safely be ignored.			
6. Wise consumers can use credit to their advantage.			
7. Buying items on credit benefits consumers more than waiting and saving for a purchase.			
8. Making the minimum payment each month is the best strategy for using a credit card.			
9. A lender has a right to ask how much a loan applicant earns each month.			
10. Declaring bankruptcy is a smart, legal way to avoid paying debts.			

Comments: _____

_____

_____

_____

_____

_____

_____

_____

(Continued on next page)

Attitude Inventory (Continued)

Rechecking Your Attitude

Directions: After completing your study of Chapter 11, respond to the Attitude Inventory statements a second time. Then compare your two sets of responses. Use the space provided at the bottom of the page to note which of your answers changed. What do you think accounts for these shifts in your opinions? Explain in the space provided.

Statement	Agree	Disagree	Undecided
1. Credit is far more important to older people than to young people and young families.			
2. Credit is easy to get if you don't need it.			
3. A good credit rating is not important to a consumer who always pays cash.			
4. A person can never have too many credit cards.			
5. The cost of credit is so small that it may safely be ignored.			
6. Wise consumers can use credit to their advantage.			
7. Buying items on credit benefits consumers more than waiting and saving for a purchase.			
8. Making the minimum payment each month is the best strategy for using a credit card.			
9. A lender has a right to ask how much a loan applicant earns each month.			
10. Declaring bankruptcy is a smart, legal way to avoid paying debts.			

Answers changed: _____

Why? _____

_____

_____

_____

_____

_____

Chapter 11 Consumer Credit

Study Guide

Directions: As you read Chapter 11, answer the following questions. Later you can use this study guide to review chapter information.

Section 11.1 Understanding Credit

1. What is credit? _____
_____
_____

2. Most credit cards provide open-end credit. What does this mean? _____
_____
_____
_____

3. How does having good credit help you obtain credit in the future? _____
_____
_____

4. Identify three types of cost involved in using credit. _____
_____
_____
_____

5. What precautions do people need to take when using credit? _____
_____
_____
_____

Section 11.2 Qualifying for Credit

6. Which of the three C's of credit has to do with reputation? What reputation do lenders look for?
_____
_____
_____

7. When asked to give credit references, what can you do if you haven't used credit before?
_____
_____
_____

(Continued on next page)

8. What is a credit bureau? _____

_____

_____

9. Where do credit bureaus get their information? _____

_____

_____

10. What can you do if you find an error in your credit report? _____

_____

_____

_____

_____

11. How can consumers who don't qualify for credit still obtain credit? _____

_____

_____

_____

Section 11.3 Managing Credit Cards

12. What is the difference between a private label credit card and a general purpose card? _____

_____

_____

_____

_____

13. In what way is a smart card different from other types of credit cards? _____

_____

_____

_____

14. Why is it a good idea to compare the APR on different revolving credit cards? _____

_____

_____

_____

15. What is the difference between a minimum payment and a credit limit? _____

_____

_____

_____

16. What is the purpose of the Truth in Lending Act? _____

_____

_____

17. Give two reasons why you should save all your credit card receipts. _____

_____

_____

18. What should you do when you receive your credit card statement? _____

_____

_____

_____

19. What action should you take if you discover an error in a credit card statement? _____

_____

_____

_____

Section 11.4 Taking Out a Loan

20. What is the difference between a home equity loan and a home improvement loan?

_____

_____

_____

_____

_____

21. Who is a greater credit risk—a typical borrower from a consumer finance company or a typical bank borrower? Why? _____

_____

_____

_____

22. What should you put in writing if you take out a private loan? _____

_____

_____

_____

(Continued on next page)

23. Why are consumers advised to avoid loan sharks? _____
_____
_____

24. Why is it best to avoid a loan that involves a balloon payment? _____
_____
_____
_____

25. What information do you need to provide when you apply for a loan? _____
_____
_____

Section 11.5 Handling Debt Problems

26. How can getting into too much debt prevent you from reaching financial goals? _____
_____
_____

27. What does repossession involve? _____
_____
_____

28. What does a collection agency do? How is the agency paid? _____
_____
_____
_____

29. List four warning signs of a debt problem. _____
_____
_____
_____
_____

30. How does a debt consolidation loan work? _____
_____
_____

31. What is a serious long-term disadvantage of declaring bankruptcy? _____
_____
_____
_____

Chapter 11 Consumer Credit

Activity

Credit Card Statement

Directions: Study the credit card monthly statement that appears below. Then answer the questions on the following page.

 Smith's Department Store

ACCOUNT SUMMARY

Previous Balance	$122.41	Credit Limit	$1500.00
Payments and Credits	$15.00	Available Credit	$1336.00
New Purchases	$53.53		
FINANCE CHARGE	$2.65	Minimum Payment Due	$16.00
New Balance	$163.59	Payment Due Date	10/14/—

To avoid additional finance charges, pay the new balance shown above by the payment due date.

ACCOUNT TRANSACTIONS

DATE	STORE	REFERENCE	DESCRIPTION	CHARGES	PAYMENTS/CREDITS
08/26	44	05250237	Budget Sportswear	$20.45	
09/02	44	05681102	Shoes	$22.58	
09/02	44	05363681	Belts	$10.50	
09/13	77		Payment – Thank You		$15.00

Billing Date	Payment Due Date	Monthly Periodic Rate	ANNUAL PERCENTAGE RATE	Average Daily Balance	Account Number
9/14/—	10/14/—	1.800%	21.60%	$146.95	12-345-678

Note: See reverse side for important information.
Questions? Call 1-800-555-1234.

Any Finance Charge added was determined by applying a 1.8% periodic rate (21.6% ANNUAL RATE) to the "Average Daily Balance." If the "Average Daily Balance" was less than $28.00 but more than zero, a minimum Finance Charge of $0.50 was applied.

To determine the "Average Daily Balance," we take the beginning balance of the account each day, add all new purchases and all billed and unpaid Finance Charges, late fees, and returned check fees, and subtract all payments, credits, and unpaid credit insurance premiums. This is the Daily Balance. The Daily Balances for all of the days in the billing cycle are added and the sum divided by the total number of days in the billing cycle. The result is the "Average Daily Balance" for the billing cycle.

(Continued on next page)

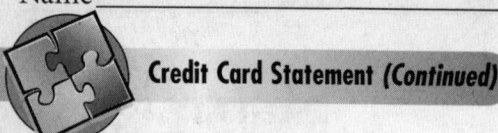
1. What type of credit card is this? How can you tell? _____
_____
_____

2. What type of credit arrangement is being offered? How can you tell? _____
_____
_____
_____
_____

3. Which of the methods described in your textbook was used to calculate the finance charge?
_____
_____

4. How much interest is the store charging, 1.8% or 21.6%? Explain. _____
_____
_____
_____

5. Suppose the balance on this account was $27 for the entire month. What would be the amount of the finance charge on the next bill? Why? _____
_____
_____
_____

6. How can the cardholder avoid paying additional finance charges? Be specific. _____
_____
_____
_____
_____

Consumer Education & Economics Student Activity Manual
Copyright © Glencoe/McGraw-Hill

Chapter 11 Consumer Credit

Credit Disclosure

Directions: You've just purchased a new video game system on credit. Below is a copy of the disclosure statement given to you by the store. Study the form. Then answer the questions on the next page.

ANNUAL PERCENTAGE RATE The cost of your credit as a yearly rate.	FINANCE CHARGE The dollar amount the credit will cost you.	AMOUNT FINANCED The amount of credit provided to you or on your behalf.	TOTAL OF PAYMENTS The amount you will have paid after you have made all payments as scheduled.	TOTAL SALE PRICE The total cost of your purchase on credit, including your downpayment of $ 25.00
14.5%	$34.66	$237.50	$272.16	$297.16

You have the right to receive at this time an itemization of the Amount Financed.

☐ I want an itemization.   ☐ I do not want an itemization.

Your payment schedule will be:

Number of Payments	Amount of Payments	When Payments are Due
12	$22.68	Monthly, beginning March 1

Insurance
Credit life insurance and credit disability insurance are not required to obtain credit, and will not be provided unless you sign and agree to pay the additional cost.

Type	Premium	Signature
Credit Life		I want credit life insurance. _____ Signature
Credit Disability		I want credit disability insurance. _____ Signature
Credit Life and Disability		I want credit life and disability insurance. _____ Signature

Security: You are giving a security interest in:
☒ the goods or property being purchased.
☐

Late Charge: If a payment is late, you will be charged $ 5.00

Prepayment: If you pay off early, you
☐ may ☒ will not have to pay a penalty.
☒ may ☐ will not be entitled to a refund of part of the finance charge.

(Continued on next page)

1. What is the monetary cost of credit in this situation? _____

2. What was the purchase price of the video game system? Explain how you arrived at that figure.

   _____

   _____

   _____

   _____

3. What is the total amount you will have paid for the game system by mid-August? Assume you make all your payments on time. Show your calculations.

   _____

   _____

4. How long will it take to pay for the game system in full? _____

5. If you are late in making a payment, how much will you be charged? _____

6. A friend of yours bought the same game system at another store. The monthly loan rate was 1.7 %. Who got the better deal—you or your friend? Explain.

   _____

   _____

   _____

   _____

7. You sell a short article to the local newspaper for $100. You would like to use the money to pay off the loan early. Will you benefit or lose by doing so? Explain.

   _____

   _____

   _____

   _____

8. The disclosure form has a space for the borrower to sign up for credit life insurance.

   a. Who pays for credit life insurance? How can you tell? _____

   _____

   _____

   b. Why do you think someone would want credit life insurance when taking out an installment loan? _____

   _____

   _____

   _____

Name_____ Date _____ Class _____

Chapter 12 Savings

Directions: Before you begin Chapter 12, take stock of your attitudes by completing the following inventory. Read each statement and check the appropriate column to indicate whether you agree, disagree, or are undecided. Use the space provided at the bottom of the page to write your comments about at least three of the statements. You will refer to this page again after completing your study of the chapter.

Statement	Agree	Disagree	Undecided
1. All families should save at least 10% of their income.			
2. Saving and investing are two different things.			
3. Saving only a small amount each week is not worthwhile.			
4. A person is more likely to save when he or she has a definite goal in mind.			
5. It's best to budget for regular expenses first and save any amount that's left over.			
6. The saying "Time is money" applies to savings accounts.			
7. People should put their savings where they can get the highest return on their money.			
8. It would be worth switching banks to get a savings account with a 1% higher interest rate.			
9. A money market account is less secure than a regular savings account.			
10. Savings bonds are risky because they are issued by the federal government rather than a bank.			

Comments: _____

_____

_____

_____

_____

_____

_____

_____

(Continued on next page)

Name_____ Date_____ Class _____

Rechecking Your Attitude

Directions: After completing your study of Chapter 12, respond to the Attitude Inventory statements a second time. Then compare your two sets of responses. Use the space provided at the bottom of the page to note which of your answers changed. What do you think accounts for these shifts in your opinions? Explain in the space provided.

Statement	Agree	Disagree	Undecided
1. All families should save at least 10% of their income.			
2. Saving and investing are two different things.			
3. Saving only a small amount each week is not worthwhile.			
4. A person is more likely to save when he or she has a definite goal in mind.			
5. It's best to budget for regular expenses first and save any amount that's left over.			
6. The saying "Time is money" applies to savings accounts.			
7. People should put their savings where they can get the highest return on their money.			
8. It would be worth switching banks to get a savings account with a 1% higher interest rate.			
9. A money market account is less secure than a regular savings account.			
10. Savings bonds are risky because they are issued by the federal government rather than a bank.			

Answers changed: _____

Why? _____

_____

_____

_____

_____

_____

Chapter 12 Savings

Directions: As you read Chapter 12, answer the following questions. Later you can use this study guide to review chapter information.

Section 12.1 The Role of Saving

1. Summarize the two ways saving can help you. _____

   _____

   _____

   _____

   _____

2. What is the difference between saving and investing? _____

   _____

   _____

   _____

   _____

3. Identify five common reasons for saving. _____

   _____

   _____

   _____

4. Why are people advised to have an emergency fund? _____

   _____

   _____

   _____

5. Give two reasons why buying an item on credit costs more than saving for the item and then

   buying it. _____

   _____

   _____

   _____

   _____

(Continued on next page)

Section 12.2 Your Savings Plan

6. What is the key to being successful at saving money? _____
_____
_____
_____

7. Once you set a specific goal for saving, how can you go about reaching that goal? _____
_____
_____
_____
_____
_____
_____

8. What is the simple principle that guides successful savings plans? What does it mean?
_____
_____
_____
_____
_____
_____

9. How does payment by direct deposit make saving easier? _____
_____
_____
_____
_____
_____
_____

Section 12.3 Earning by Saving

10. Briefly explain the difference between simple interest and compound interest. _____
_____
_____
_____
_____

11. What does the annual percentage yield (APY) of an account tell you? _____
_____
_____

12. Why is it said that "time is money" when it comes to saving or investing? _____
_____
_____
_____

13. What does the rule of 72 tell you? _____
_____
_____
_____

Section 12.4 Savings Options

14. Why do you need to check on the safety of individual accounts offered by a financial institution?
_____
_____
_____

15. What does the term liquidity refer to? _____
_____
_____
_____

16. Give three examples of restrictions that might apply to a savings product. _____
_____
_____
_____
_____
_____

(Continued on next page)

Study Guide *(Continued)*

17. Which is generally the most liquid savings option? What is one drawback of this option?

_____

_____

_____

18. What kinds of restrictions might a money market account have? _____

_____

_____

_____

_____

_____

_____

19. Why should you avoid withdrawing money from a CD before the end of its term?

_____

_____

_____

_____

_____

_____

_____

_____

20. Identify two benefits of buying savings bonds. _____

_____

_____

_____

_____

_____

_____

_____

Chapter 12 Savings

So You Want to Be a Millionaire?

Directions: Unless you win the lottery or a game show, having a million dollars may seem impossible. Yet it's possible to become a millionaire through steady savings—and unlike participants in a lottery or a game show, everyone who follows this strategy can win. Study the table below, then answer the questions that follow.

Initial Deposit	Interest Rate (Compounded Daily)	Amount Added Weekly	Number of Years to Become a Millionaire
$500	5%	$100	47.2
$500	5%	$200	35.2
$500	8%	$100	34.9
$500	8%	$200	27.0
$500	10%	$100	30.0
$500	10%	$200	23.6
$1000	5%	$100	47.1
$1000	5%	$200	35.1
$1000	8%	$100	34.8
$1000	8%	$200	27.0
$1000	10%	$100	29.9
$1000	10%	$200	23.5
$5000	5%	$100	46.4
$5000	5%	$200	34.8
$5000	8%	$100	34.1
$5000	8%	$200	26.6
$5000	10%	$100	29.2
$5000	10%	$200	23.2

1. Among the possibilities listed in the table, which plan would yield a million dollars most quickly?

_____

_____

2. Suppose you make an initial deposit of $1,000 and earn 5% interest. If you add $200 per week, how many years sooner would you reach your goal than if you added only $100 per week?

_____

3. Suppose you make a $100 weekly deposit at 5%. If you start with $5,000, how much sooner would you reach your goal than if you started with only $1,000?

_____

(Continued on next page)

4. Compare your answers to items 2 and 3. In which case does changing the savings strategy make the most difference in how soon you reach your goal? Why is this true?

_____

_____

_____

5. If you add $200 per week to your account, how much will you have added in a year?

_____

6. Predict how the outcome would be affected if you waited until the end of the year to deposit the amount in item 5 instead of adding $200 per week. Explain your reasoning.

_____

_____

_____

_____

7. Of the types of savings options discussed in Section 12.4, which would allow you to add money each week?

_____

_____

_____

8. Savings accounts tend to have lower interest rates than many other savings and investment options. How could you take advantage of the convenience of a savings account, but earn a greater return overall?

_____

_____

_____

9. What would be the advantage of using payroll deductions to buy savings bonds?

_____

_____

_____

_____

Chapter 13 Investments

Attitude Inventory

Directions: Before you begin Chapter 13, take stock of your attitudes by completing the following inventory. Read each statement and check the appropriate column to indicate whether you agree, disagree, or are undecided. Use the space provided at the bottom of the page to write your comments about at least three of the statements. You will refer to this page again after completing your study of the chapter.

Statement	Agree	Disagree	Undecided
1. Investing money is for rich people.			
2. A knowledge of investment opportunities should be part of every person's basic education.			
3. There is no difference between investing and gambling.			
4. Consumers should not depend on Social Security for their retirement income.			
5. An individual risks more by investing in corporate stocks than by putting money in a savings account.			
6. The key to investing in the stock market is to rely on the advice of a good broker.			
7. A mutual fund is a good choice only if you have a large amount of money to invest.			
8. Buying rare baseball cards is a good investment.			
9. Most people don't need to prepare a will before age 60.			
10. Funerals should be planned and paid for in advance.			

Comments: _____

_____

_____

_____

_____

_____

_____

(Continued on next page)

Name _____ Date _____ Class _____

Rechecking Your Attitude

Directions: After completing your study of Chapter 13, respond to the Attitude Inventory statements a second time. Then compare your two sets of responses. Use the space provided at the bottom of the page to note which of your answers changed. What do you think accounts for these shifts in your opinions? Explain in the space provided.

Statement	Agree	Disagree	Undecided
1. Investing money is for rich people.			
2. A knowledge of investment opportunities should be part of every person's basic education.			
3. There is no difference between investing and gambling.			
4. Consumers should not depend on Social Security for their retirement income.			
5. An individual risks more by investing in corporate stocks than by putting money in a savings account.			
6. The key to investing in the stock market is to rely on the advice of a good broker.			
7. A mutual fund is a good choice only if you have a large amount of money to invest.			
8. Buying rare baseball cards is a good investment.			
9. Most people don't need to prepare a will before age 60.			
10. Funerals should be planned and paid for in advance.			

Answers changed: _____

Why? _____

_____

_____

_____

_____

_____

_____

_____

Consumer Education & Economics Student Activity Manual
Copyright © Glencoe/McGraw-Hill

Chapter 13 Investments

Directions: As you read Chapter 13, answer the following questions. Later you can use this study guide to review chapter information.

Section 13.1 Investment Strategies

1. What is investing? _____

_____

_____

2. List the four basic characteristics by which investments are judged. _____

_____

_____

3. What does the term *volatile* mean when applied to investments? _____

_____

4. Identify three types of investment strategies. _____

_____

5. What does diversification involve? Why is it advised? _____

_____

_____

_____

6. What is asset allocation? _____

_____

_____

Section 13.2 Retirement Planning

7. Identify three factors that influence the amount of Social Security benefits you receive.

_____

_____

8. What is the key difference between a defined-benefit pension plan and a defined-contribution pension plan? _____

_____

_____

_____

(Continued on next page)

9. What is a 401(k) plan? _____
   _____
   _____

10. Summarize the main differences between a traditional IRA and a Roth IRA. _____
    _____
    _____
    _____
    _____

11. What category of workers might set up a Keogh plan? _____
    _____

12. You review your retirement plan and find that your anticipated needs exceed your anticipated retirement fund. What actions can you take? _____
    _____
    _____
    _____
    _____
    _____

Section 13.3 The Stock Market

13. What is the difference between the stock market and a stock exchange? _____
    _____
    _____

14. Name the two largest stock exchanges in the United States. _____
    _____
    _____

15. How does the Securities and Exchange Commission protect investors? _____
    _____
    _____

16. What is a dividend? How often are dividends usually paid? _____
    _____
    _____
    _____

Consumer Education & Economics Student Activity Manual
Copyright © Glencoe/McGraw-Hill

17. What is the difference between a full-service broker and a discount broker? _____

_____

_____

_____

_____

18. Identify four factors that influence a stock's price. _____

_____

_____

_____

19. What are blue chip stocks? Why are they considered to be lower in risk than other stocks?

_____

_____

_____

_____

20. What kinds of information does a company's annual report provide? _____

_____

_____

_____

_____

Section 13.4 Other Investments

21. Describe the two ways that bonds provide a return. _____

_____

_____

_____

22. What does a bond's level of risk depend on? _____

_____

_____

_____

(Continued on next page)

23. What is a mutual fund? _____
_____
_____

24. What are the two key advantages that mutual funds have over individual stocks and bonds?
_____
_____

25. Which type of stock fund normally holds the highest risk? _____
_____

26. What can you do to investigate a mutual fund? _____
_____
_____

Section 13.5 Estate Planning

27. What is estate planning? _____
_____
_____
_____

28. Summarize the benefits of estate planning. _____
_____
_____
_____

29. Identify the four basic functions of a will. _____
_____
_____
_____
_____

30. What is the difference between a living trust and a living will? _____
_____
_____
_____
_____

Chapter 13 Investments

Who's Investing Wisely?

Directions: The investors described below all believe they are following a sound investment plan. However, some of them could benefit from knowledgeable advice. For each situation, explain either why you think the investment strategy is wise or why you think it should be changed.

1. Harrison has several friends who are knowledgeable about investing, including one who is a broker. At a party last week, Harrison overheard his friends discussing real estate investment trusts. They were very enthusiastic about this form of investment. Harrison couldn't follow the details of their conversation, since he doesn't understand how real estate investment trusts work. However, he has confidence in his friends' judgment and has decided to invest $5,000.

   _____

   _____

   _____

   _____

2. Josh is dissatisfied with the low interest rate his savings account is earning. He has decided to withdraw most of the money and invest it. He has read about people who were able to make a huge profit by collecting old toys that went way up in value. Josh figures he will start buying old toys at garage sales and flea markets. If he ever needs money quickly, he can always sell the toys; meanwhile, he will enjoy displaying his collection.

   _____

   _____

   _____

   _____

3. For about five years, Cassandra has been investing in a mutual fund that tracks the performance of the Standard & Poor's 500 index. In the last year, the value of the S&P 500 has gone steadily down. Meanwhile, Cassandra has not changed her investment strategy. She continues to buy more shares in the mutual fund and does not plan to sell any in the near future; in fact, she intends to hang on to this investment for the next 15 or 20 years. She reasons that while the index is down, she is getting a good bargain on the shares she buys.

   _____

   _____

   _____

   _____

(Continued on next page)

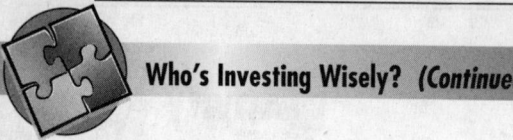

4. Hector and Lisa are in their early 30s and have well-defined goals for saving and investing. First, they are focusing on accumulating money in a savings account for emergencies. Then they will save up for the down payment on a car, which they plan to buy in three years. They feel the stock market is too risky for this money, so they will put it in certificates of deposit and Treasury bills. Next, they will put aside $2,000 per year toward a down payment on a home, which they hope to buy in 10 or 12 years. They think a conservative mutual fund might be a good place to accumulate funds for their home, but they will investigate their options further when the time comes. Finally, after purchasing their home, Hector and Lisa will set up IRA accounts for retirement. The IRA accounts will be invested in a balanced portfolio of stocks and bonds.

_____

_____

_____

_____

_____

_____

5. Maureen started her first full-time job a year ago. She works for a major, well-established corporation and is now eligible for the company's 401(k) plan. She has decided to contribute the maximum amount to take advantage of the tax benefits and to get a head start on investing for retirement. According to the plan, the company's 3% match is automatically invested in the company's stock. Maureen is very familiar with the industry in which she works and has been researching facts and figures about her corporation's financial health. She feels the company is well managed and the stock offers excellent prospects for long-term growth. Several financial ratings services agree with her. Based on her research, Maureen has decided to invest her contribution in the company's stock.

_____

_____

_____

_____

_____

_____

Chapter 14 Insurance

Directions: Before you begin Chapter 14, take stock of your attitudes by completing the following inventory. Read each statement and check the appropriate column to indicate whether you agree, disagree, or are undecided. Use the space provided at the bottom of the page to write your comments about at least three of the statements. You will refer to this page again after completing your study of the chapter.

Statement	Agree	Disagree	Undecided
1. Most people need more insurance than they have.			
2. Insurance companies get rich at the expense of consumers.			
3. The government should provide insurance protection for those who cannot afford it.			
4. The least expensive insurance policy is the best choice.			
5. If you never have an accident, auto insurance is a waste of money.			
6. It's unfair that auto insurance rates are higher for teens than for adults.			
7. Renters don't need home insurance.			
8. Rising health care costs are the fault of doctors.			
9. Consumers are better off with traditional health insurance than with an HMO.			
10. Everyone should have life insurance.			

Comments: _____

_____

_____

_____

_____

_____

_____

(Continued on next page)

Rechecking Your Attitude

Directions: After completing your study of Chapter 14, respond to the Attitude Inventory statements a second time. Then compare your two sets of responses. Use the space provided at the bottom of the page to note which of your answers changed. What do you think accounts for these shifts in your opinions? Explain in the space provided.

Statement	Agree	Disagree	Undecided
1. Most people need more insurance than they have.			
2. Insurance companies get rich at the expense of consumers.			
3. The government should provide insurance protection for those who cannot afford it.			
4. The least expensive insurance policy is the best choice.			
5. If you never have an accident, auto insurance is a waste of money.			
6. It's unfair that auto insurance rates are higher for teens than for adults.			
7. Renters don't need home insurance.			
8. Rising health care costs are the fault of doctors.			
9. Consumers are better off with traditional health insurance than with an HMO.			
10. Everyone should have life insurance.			

Answers changed: _____

Why? _____

_____

_____

_____

_____

_____

_____

_____

Chapter 14 Insurance

Study Guide

Directions: As you read Chapter 14, answer the following questions. Later you can use this study guide to review chapter information.

Section 14.1 How Insurance Works

1. Identify the three broad categories of risk that can cause financial loss. _____
    _____
    _____
    _____

2. How does insurance protect you? _____
    _____
    _____

3. What is the difference between exclusions and endorsements in an insurance policy?
    _____
    _____
    _____
    _____

4. What is a deductible? Why do insurance companies include deductibles in their policies?
    _____
    _____
    _____
    _____
    _____

5. What are the four types of insurance that most people have? _____
    _____
    _____
    _____

Section 14.2 Auto Insurance

6. What does a no-fault insurance system place limits on? _____
    _____
    _____

7. List three factors that contribute to the depreciation of a vehicle. _____
    _____
    _____
    _____

(Continued on next page)

Study Guide *(Continued)*

8. What does the liability portion of auto insurance cover? _____
_____
_____

9. Under what circumstances might you decide to drop collision and comprehensive coverage?
_____
_____

10. Why do people who live in large cities pay more for car insurance than those in suburban and rural areas? _____
_____
_____

11. What are the first things you should do if you are involved in an accident? _____
_____
_____

12. What kinds of information should you exchange with other drivers if you are involved in an accident? _____
_____
_____

Section 14.3 Home Insurance

13. In home insurance, what is the difference between property coverage and liability coverage?
_____
_____
_____
_____

14. What does a condominium owner's insurance cover? _____
_____
_____

15. Why do you have to pay a higher premium for replacement value coverage? _____
_____
_____

16. Identify the three types of liability coverage offered under a home insurance policy. _____
_____
_____
_____

17. List four factors that might affect a person's home insurance rates. _____
_____
_____
_____

18. What purpose does a household inventory serve? _____
_____
_____
_____

Section 14.4 Health Insurance

19. List six kinds of coverage that might be included in a health care plan. _____
_____
_____
_____

20. What is the purpose of major medical coverage? _____
_____
_____

21. What is the purpose of the COBRA plan? _____
_____
_____
_____

22. How does a fee-for-service plan work? _____
_____
_____
_____

23. Identify the three most common types of managed care plan. _____
_____
_____
_____

24. In what ways does a point-of-service plan provide more choice than an HMO? _____
_____
_____
_____

(Continued on next page)

25. What is the purpose of the Medicaid program? _____

_____

_____

_____

Section 14.5 Life Insurance

26. What is term life insurance? What is its main advantage over other forms of life insurance?

_____

_____

_____

_____

27. Identify four different forms of permanent life insurance. _____

_____

_____

_____

28. Which form of life insurance allows you to have control over how the cash value is invested?

_____

_____

29. In a life insurance policy, what does the term *beneficiary* refer to? _____

_____

_____

_____

30. What factors do insurance companies look at when determining the cost of an individual's life insurance policy? _____

_____

_____

_____

Chapter 14 Insurance

Finding an Agent

Directions: Kim and Paul Takimoto want to find a new insurance agent. For each situation described below, decide whether you would consider buying insurance from the agent. In each case, briefly explain your choice.

1. Paul tries calling Agent 1 four times. The first three times he gets a busy signal; the fourth time, an answering service. He leaves a message, but his call is never returned.

   _____

   _____

   _____

   _____

2. When Paul calls Agent 2, he gets voice mail and leaves a message. Early that evening, the agent calls back. She asks Paul a long list of questions about his insurance needs. The she requests a few days to "get together some possibilities." They agree to meet at Paul's home later that week.

   _____

   _____

   _____

   _____

   _____

3. Kim gets Agent 3 on the phone on the first try. The agent asks several questions about their insurance needs and promises to call back the next day. She does. The premiums she quotes, however, seem high. When Kim inquires about the most cost-efficient coverage, Agent 3 responds, "No one can ever have too much insurance."

   _____

   _____

   _____

   _____

   _____

(Continued on next page)

4. Agent 4 quotes similarly high premiums. When Paul and Kim question the figures, the agent suggests that they are "not familiar with real-world costs these days." When Kim offers some cost-cutting suggestions, the agent implies that she doesn't understand how insurance works. The agent leaves his figures with Paul and Kim and tells them to "get in touch if you're interested."

_____

_____

_____

_____

5. After a brief initial phone contact, Agent 5 meets Paul and Kim for breakfast one morning before work. They do the survey on insurance needs over their meal, and the agent gives them some brochures describing basic coverages. He singles out two dealing with economy plans. The examples, he admits, are not totally accurate for their situation. If they are genuinely interested, however, the agent promises to work up detailed figures. He also describes some features (like flood insurance) that no other agent has mentioned.

_____

_____

_____

_____

_____

_____

_____

Chapter 14 Insurance

Auto Coverage

Directions: Read the following story, then complete the items that follow.

When Mario drives, he likes to speed and weave in and out of traffic. One day the traffic stopped and Mario didn't. He slammed into a brand new car. The car he hit was totaled and its occupants, Sam and Mary, were severely injured. Bad as the accident was, Mario was not concerned. His injuries were minor and his insurance, he was sure, would pay for everything. Was he right?

1. Mario carried 20/40/15 coverage, the state minimum. Damages were assessed as shown below, and Mario was held fully responsible. Who paid what? Complete the chart.

Coverage	Limit	Court Award	Insurance Pays	Mario Pays
Bodily Injury	$_____ per person	Sam: $95,000	$_____	$_____
	$_____ per accident	Mary: $20,000	$_____	$_____
Property Damage	$_____ per accident	Sam: $25,000	$_____	$_____
TOTAL		$140,000	$_____	$_____

2. Suppose Mario's policy limits had been 100/300/50. Would it have made any difference in his personal liability? To find out, complete the chart.

Coverage	Limit	Court Award	Insurance Pays	Mario Pays
Bodily Injury	$_____ per person	Sam: $95,000	$_____	$_____
	$_____ per accident	Mary: $20,000	$_____	$_____
Property Damage	$_____ per accident	Sam: $25,000	$_____	$_____
TOTAL		$140,000	$_____	$_____

 **Activity**

Chapter 14 Insurance

Property Coverage

Directions: Review the different forms of home insurance described in your textbook. In the chart below, place a checkmark under each type of policy that would cover the situation described in the left column. Remember that some situations may be covered by more than one type of insurance policy.

Situation	HO-1	HO-2	HO-3	Flood Insurance	Earthquake Insurance
1. A neighbor's five-year-old son drives the family car through your front-yard fence.					
2. A tornado levels the house.					
3. A helicopter crash-lands on your garage.					
4. Your hot-water tank ruptures, flooding the basement recreation room.					
5. While you're away one weekend, thieves pull a moving van up to your house and empty it of all furniture, appliances, and personal belongings.					
6. During a winter storm, the back porch collapses from the weight of accumulated ice and snow.					
7. A sinkhole mysteriously appears in your backyard and swallows up the tool shed and patio.					
8. During an earthquake, a hillside slips and demolishes one wing of your house.					
9. Neighborhood children playing with fire-crackers set the roof ablaze.					
10. An explosion in a manufacturing plant several blocks away shatters every window in your house.					
11. Subzero temperatures cause the household water pipes to freeze and burst.					
12. An earthen dam located in the hills above your town gives way, flooding the whole community.					

Name_____ Date _____ Class _____

Chapter 15 Persuasion in the Marketplace

Directions: Before you begin Chapter 15, take stock of your attitudes by completing the following inventory. Read each statement and check the appropriate column to indicate whether you agree, disagree, or are undecided. Use the space provided at the bottom of the page to write your comments about at least three of the statements. You will refer to this page again after completing your study of the chapter.

Statement	Agree	Disagree	Undecided
1. Most product advertising contains too much exaggeration and misinformation to be helpful.			
2. Advertising is generally effective in persuading consumers to buy products.			
3. The Internet should be free of advertising.			
4. Most advertisements appeal to consumers' reason and judgment.			
5. A salesperson who tries to interest you in a more expensive item is just doing his or her job.			
6. Information on a tag such as "Compare at $30" is helpful to the consumer.			
7. You cannot trust a salesperson to tell you the truth.			
8. Smart consumers always buy items on sale.			
9. Clipping coupons is time well spent.			
10. Telemarketing should be banned.			

Comments: _____

_____

_____

_____

_____

_____

_____

_____

(Continued on next page)

Rechecking Your Attitude

Directions: After completing your study of Chapter 15, respond to the Attitude Inventory statements a second time. Then compare your two sets of responses. Use the space provided at the bottom of the page to note which of your answers changed. What do you think accounts for these shifts in your opinions? Explain in the space provided.

Statement	Agree	Disagree	Undecided
1. Most product advertising contains too much exaggeration and misinformation to be helpful.			
2. Advertising is generally effective in persuading consumers to buy products.			
3. The Internet should be free of advertising.			
4. Most advertisements appeal to consumers' reason and judgment.			
5. A salesperson who tries to interest you in a more expensive item is just doing his or her job.			
6. Information on a tag such as "Compare at $30" is helpful to the consumer.			
7. You cannot trust a salesperson to tell you the truth.			
8. Smart consumers always buy items on sale.			
9. Clipping coupons is time well spent.			
10. Telemarketing should be banned.			

Answers changed: _____

Why? _____

_____

_____

_____

_____

_____

_____

Chapter 15 Persuasion in the Marketplace

Study Guide

Directions: As you read Chapter 15, answer the following questions. Later you can use this study guide to review chapter information.

Section 15.1 The Role of Advertising

1. List six examples of advertising methods. _____
    _____
    _____
    _____

2. How does advertising help newspapers, television stations, and other media? _____
    _____
    _____

3. Why is advertising's power of persuasion considered by some to be a drawback? _____
    _____
    _____
    _____

4. What is the purpose of FTC regulation of advertising? _____
    _____

Section 15.2 Evaluating Advertisements

5. Why do you need to recognize the strategies that advertisers use? _____
    _____
    _____

6. What is puffery? Why is it not considered to be deceptive? _____
    _____
    _____
    _____
    _____

7. What do FTC rules governing endorsements by individuals aim to do? _____
    _____
    _____
    _____
    _____

(Continued on next page)

8. What is the difference between the bandwagon technique of advertising and the trendsetter technique? _____

_____

_____

_____

9. Why is it essential for consumers to be able to recognize advertising? _____

_____

_____

10. Why do you need to ask yourself what an advertisement is *not* telling you? _____

_____

_____

_____

Section 15.3 Promotional and Sales Tactics

11. Why do retailers hold clearance sales? _____

_____

12. What is a rain check? _____

_____

_____

13. What is a loss leader? Why do retailers sell loss leaders? _____

_____

_____

_____

14. What is the usual way a consumer receives a rebate? _____

_____

_____

15. What does wise use of coupons entail? _____

_____

_____

_____

16. What does the sales technique known as trading up involve? _____

_____

_____

_____

Name_____ Date_____ Class _____

Chapter 15 Persuasion in the Marketplace

Evaluating Ad Claims

Directions: Ads are often written in a way that makes a product or offer sound better than it really is. For example, an ad may imply more than is actually stated, make vague claims or meaningless comparisons, or state opinion rather than fact. Your critical thinking skills can help you recognize these tactics. Suppose you encountered the following phrases in ads. In the space provided, write your critical analysis of each ad's claims.

1. "A $79 value…Our price $39.95." _____

_____

_____

_____

_____

_____

2. "With Texarcon you get more miles per gallon." _____

_____

_____

_____

_____

_____

3. "Comes in Large, Extra Large, and Jumbo sizes." _____

_____

_____

_____

_____

_____

4. "Hair Repair will restore that baby-soft silkiness to your hair or your money back." _____

_____

_____

_____

_____

(Continued on next page)

Consumer Education & Economics Student Activity Manual
Copyright © Glencoe/McGraw-Hill

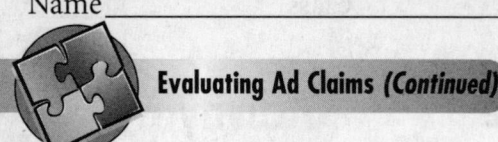

5. "The honey made nature's way." _____

_____

_____

_____

6. "10% off our low everyday prices." _____

_____

_____

_____

_____

_____

_____

7. "Unbelievable savings on imported cameras!" _____

_____

_____

_____

_____

_____

_____

8. "Extra-strength Puff-Stuff has more softening power than the two leading brands combined."

_____

_____

_____

_____

_____

_____

Chapter 15 Persuasion in the Marketplace

Activity

Product Promotions

Directions: Marketers use many kinds of promotional methods to entice consumers to buy. Smart consumers think about whether promotions offer them real value. Read the following sales pitches and answer the questions as directed.

1. "Hello, I'm calling on behalf of the Clearglass Window Company. You've been specially selected to receive two replacement windows absolutely free just for buying six additional windows."

   a. How is the wording of this offer designed to appeal to consumers?

   _____

   _____

   b. What criteria do you think were used to select consumers for the special window offer?

   _____

   _____

   _____

   c. If you heard this sales pitch, what would you want to consider or investigate before accepting the offer?

   _____

   _____

   _____

2. "Sign up for the Prestige credit card and receive a free Prestige windbreaker—a $60 value! (Available in red XL only.)"

   a. When evaluating the offer of the free windbreaker, what questions might consumers want to ask themselves? Name at least three.

   _____

   _____

   _____

   b. What selling points of a credit card might offer more real value to consumers than the promise of a free windbreaker?

   _____

   _____

   _____

(Continued on next page)

3. "March Super Sale!! Prices slashed on all skis, ice skates, and sleds! Save up to 40% now!"

    a. Do you think this offer provides real value for consumers? Explain.

    _____

    _____

    _____

    b. What is the major drawback of this offer?

    _____

    _____

    _____

    c. What could consumers do to make sure they benefit from the offer in spite of its drawbacks?

    _____

    _____

    _____

4. Suppose Yummy brand macaroni and cheese is on sale this week at B & C Supermarket. The 6-oz. box is 75 cents and the 12-oz. box is 99 cents. You have two coupons, each good for 25 cents off any two boxes of the product. You also have a mail-in rebate form good for $2 if you send in four proofs of purchase from any size Yummy macaroni and cheese. On Tuesdays, B & C Supermarket doubles the face value of manufacturer's coupons up to 50 cents. Explain how to pay as little as possible for macaroni and cheese. In the box provided, show your calculation for the final cost to you.

    _____

    _____

    _____

Consumer Education & Economics Student Activity Manual
Copyright © Glencoe/McGraw-Hill

Chapter 16 Shopping Skills

Attitude Inventory

Directions: Before you begin Chapter 16, take stock of your attitudes by completing the following inventory. Read each statement and check the appropriate column to indicate whether you agree, disagree, or are undecided. Use the space provided at the bottom of the page to write your comments about at least three of the statements. You will refer to this page again after completing your study of the chapter.

Statement	Agree	Disagree	Undecided
1. Shopping in discount stores is a mistake—you get what you pay for.			
2. Most sellers at online auction sites are trustworthy.			
3. Shopping on the Internet is a good way to find bargains.			
4. Shopping at home is preferable to shopping in stores.			
5. If you're unhappy with a purchase, you can always get your money back as long as the product has a warranty.			
6. Paying extra for a service contract is usually worthwhile.			
7. Consumers should always take the time to shop at several stores and compare prices.			
8. Products with well-known brand names are generally higher in quality than generic products.			
9. If you want to hire someone to perform a service, you should ask friends for recommendations.			
10. If you're dissatisfied with a service, you should refuse to pay for it.			

Comments: _____

_____

_____

_____

_____

_____

_____

_____

(Continued on next page)

Consumer Education & Economics Student Activity Manual
Copyright © Glencoe/McGraw-Hill

 **Attitude Inventory** *(Continued)*

Rechecking Your Attitude

Directions: After completing your study of Chapter 16, respond to the Attitude Inventory statements a second time. Then compare your two sets of responses. Use the space provided at the bottom of the page to note which of your answers changed. What do you think accounts for these shifts in your opinions? Explain in the space provided.

Statement	Agree	Disagree	Undecided
1. Shopping in discount stores is a mistake—you get what you pay for.			
2. Most sellers at online auction sites are trustworthy.			
3. Shopping on the Internet is a good way to find bargains.			
4. Shopping at home is preferable to shopping in stores.			
5. If you're unhappy with a purchase, you can always get your money back as long as the product has a warranty.			
6. Paying extra for a service contract is usually worthwhile.			
7. Consumers should always take the time to shop at several stores and compare prices.			
8. Products with well-known brand names are generally higher in quality than generic products.			
9. If you want to hire someone to perform a service, you should ask friends for recommendations.			
10. If you're dissatisfied with a service, you should refuse to pay for it.			

Answers changed: _____

Why? _____

_____

_____

_____

_____

_____

Consumer Education & Economics Student Activity Manual
Copyright © Glencoe/McGraw-Hill

Chapter 16 Shopping Skills

Directions: As you read Chapter 16, answer the following questions. Later you can use this study guide to review chapter information.

Section 16.1 Your Shopping Options

1. In what ways do retailers differ from one another? _____

_____

_____

_____

2. What information can a Better Business Bureau provide about a retailer that interests you?

_____

_____

_____

_____

_____

3. How does shopping on the Internet save you time and trouble? _____

_____

_____

_____

_____

_____

4. What two actions should you take before providing your credit card number to an online shopping site? _____

_____

_____

_____

5. Why is it important to read the seller's feedback rating when bidding on an Internet auction?

_____

_____

_____

_____

(Continued on next page)

Section 16.2 Understanding Warranties

6. What is a warranty? What is its purpose? _____

_____

_____

_____

_____

7. In implied warranties, what is merchantability? _____

_____

_____

_____

8. What is the purpose of the Magnuson-Moss Warranty Act? _____

_____

_____

_____

_____

9. What is a full warranty? _____

_____

_____

_____

_____

10. When you buy a product that comes with a warranty, what should you do with the warranty?

_____

_____

_____

11. What should you do if your complaint about a warranty is not adequately addressed?

_____

_____

_____

12. What is a service contract? _____

_____

_____

_____

13. Why do many experts advise against buying a service contract? _____

_____

_____

_____

_____

_____

Section 16.3 Finding the Best Buys

14. When considering your budget for a particular purchase, what factors should you take into account? _____

_____

_____

_____

_____

_____

_____

15. When researching a product, what special information can you get from consumer magazines?

_____

_____

_____

_____

16. How can you research products when visiting stores? _____

_____

_____

_____

_____

_____

_____

(Continued on next page)

17. What are the three main strategies for comparison shopping? _____

_____

_____

_____

18. Which are usually more expensive—national brands or store brands? Why? _____

_____

_____

_____

Section 16.4 Shopping for Services

19. Why is it harder to comparison shop when buying a service rather than a product? _____

_____

_____

20. How can you identify candidates for a service job? _____

_____

_____

_____

_____

21. What can you learn by talking to references given by a service provider? _____

_____

_____

_____

_____

22. Why is it a good idea to get an estimate before agreeing to have service work done? _____

_____

_____

_____

_____

Chapter 16 Shopping Skills

Activity

Buying Options

Directions: If you were shopping for the items listed below, where would you be most likely to purchase them? Where would you be least likely to spend your money? Consider local retail stores, warehouse clubs, factory outlets, television home shopping services, catalogs, and the Internet. Write your choices in the space provided and explain your reasons.

1. Glassware for wedding gift

    Most likely: _____

    Least likely: _____

    Explanation: _____

2. Expansion card for computer

    Most likely: _____

    Least likely: _____

    Explanation: _____

3. Bath towels

    Most likely: _____

    Least likely: _____

    Explanation: _____

4. Barbecue grill

    Most likely: _____

    Least likely: _____

    Explanation: _____

5. Swimwear

    Most likely: _____

    Least likely: _____

    Explanation: _____

6. Record album from the '60s

    Most likely: _____

    Least likely: _____

    Explanation: _____

 **Activity**

Chapter 16 Shopping Skills

Home Shopping Advice

Directions: Imagine that you write a consumer advice column that appears in newspapers around the country. This week's column focuses on home shopping problems that readers have encountered. Read each reader's letter below and write your response in the space provided. If necessary, use an additional sheet of paper.

1. I've spent a lot of time watching TV shopping channels while I've been recuperating from surgery. The hosts of the segments are so personable, and some of the products are very nice, but I'd be embarrassed if anyone knew how much I've spent on products that I really don't need. Do you have any tips for me?

   _____

   _____

   _____

   _____

   _____

2. I have a watch that I bought online, and I want to return it. The problem is I didn't have time to open the package before I left on a trip for my school's foreign exchange program. While I was traveling, I bought a watch that I like much better. Now more than a month has passed, and the company won't allow me to return the watch. Can you help me?

   _____

   _____

   _____

   _____

3. I ordered a croquet set from a mail-order catalog in June. It was supposed to be here in two weeks. Now it's August and the set is still on back order. I'm afraid summer will be over by the time it gets here. Can I cancel the order at this point?

   _____

   _____

   _____

   _____

4. I need a new monitor for my computer. I found the model I want online for $25 less than at a computer store here in town. Shipping and handling costs $14.95, though. What would you do?

   _____

   _____

   _____

   _____

Chapter 16 Shopping Skills

Understanding Warranties

Directions: You belong to a small band that plays for dances and school activities. You just received a new electronic keyboard for your birthday. The keyboard is made by the Matsuda Company and comes with an eight-page owner's manual, which contains the following statement. Read it carefully. Then answer the questions that follow.

Limited Warranty

Matsuda Corporation warrants that this electronic keyboard is and shall remain free of defects in materials and workmanship for a period of one year from the date of original purchase. This warranty excludes damage or wear resulting from accident, abuse, tampering, unauthorized repair, power surges, or failure to follow the Standard Operating Instructions listed in the Owner's Manual.

If your electronic keyboard fails to operate under normal use conditions within the warranty period, Matsuda will repair or replace it at their discretion. Repairs will be made using new or thoroughly reconditioned parts, also at Matsuda's discretion.

Send the product, at your own expense, to Matsuda Corporation, 348 Wilson Drive, Kenosha, WI 53142, or hand carry it to your nearest Matsuda-approved service center (see page 5 of your Owner's Manual). If shipping, include a note stating your name and address, the nature of the defect or malfunction, and the date of purchase. NOTE: Masuda will not be responsible for shipping damage. Therefore, when sending your product for service, use a sturdy box, pack securely, and insure your package against damage or loss in transit.

No charge will be made for repairs to defective parts under this warranty. Before authorizing or completing such repairs, however, Matsuda may require proof of purchase in the form of an original sales receipt or copy thereof. A minimum period of six to eight weeks shall be deemed reasonable for all repairs. Any return shipping charges will be borne by Matsuda.

The remedies described in this warranty are exclusive. Matsuda shall not be liable for indirect or consequential damages.

This warranty gives you specific legal rights. You may, however, have other rights, which vary from state to state. Some states do not allow limitations on how long an implied warranty lasts or on indirect or consequential damages. Therefore, the above limitations or exclusions may not apply to you.

---

1. Why is this identified as a limited warranty rather than a full warranty? _____
_____
_____
_____

2. Against what types of problems is the owner protected? _____
_____

(Continued on next page)

3. What types of problems are specifically excluded from warranty protection? _____

_____

_____

4. What is the length of the warranty? _____

5. What remedies are available to the purchaser of a defective keyboard? _____

_____

_____

6. Analyze the following situations. Would the incident described be covered under the warranty provisions? Why or why not?

   a. When you set your keyboard to play accompanying drums, you get a humming noise but no drums. For repair, you return the keyboard to the dealer from which it was purchased.

   _____

   _____

   b. Instead of taking your electronic keyboard to a service center, you mail it C.O.D. to the address given in the warranty.

   _____

   _____

   c. You don't like the idea of Matsuda using reconditioned parts for repairs. You send the keyboard (postage paid) to Kenosha, but in your letter you request that only new parts be used as replacements.

   _____

   _____

   _____

   d. Your keyboard develops a minor problem, so you mail it to Kenosha. Although you packed the keyboard carefully, you are informed that it was damaged when it arrived. You ask Matsuda to send you a new keyboard.

   _____

   _____

   _____

   e. The plug on your keyboard proves to be defective. The result is a small fire and large bill for rewiring the wall outlet. You send the bill to Matsuda.

   _____

   _____

   _____

   _____

Chapter 17 Technology Products

Attitude Inventory

Directions: Before you begin Chapter 17, take stock of your attitudes by completing the following inventory. Read each statement and check the appropriate column to indicate whether you agree, disagree, or are undecided. Use the space provided at the bottom of the page to write your comments about at least three of the statements. You will refer to this page again after completing your study of the chapter.

Statement	Agree	Disagree	Undecided
1. If a person finds computers hard to use, it's because he or she isn't smart enough.			
2. For most people, having a wireless phone or pager is essential.			
3. Consumers should expect to replace high-tech products every two to three years to keep up with new technology.			
4. The more features and capabilities an electronic product has, the better.			
5. Since technology is constantly changing, consumers must rely on the recommendations of expert salespeople.			
6. Shopping for a wireless phone is confusing because so many different plans are offered.			
7. When different companies compete to provide local and long distance phone service, consumers benefit.			
8. The government should ensure that all citizens have access to the Internet.			
9. Whatever type of computer is used by the majority of people must be the best choice.			
10. A used computer might meet a consumer's needs just as well as a new one.			

Comments: _____
_____
_____
_____
_____
_____

(Continued on next page)

Consumer Education & Economics Student Activity Manual
Copyright © Glencoe/McGraw-Hill

Rechecking Your Attitude

Directions: After completing your study of Chapter 17, respond to the Attitude Inventory statements a second time. Then compare your two sets of responses. Use the space provided at the bottom of the page to note which of your answers changed. What do you think accounts for these shifts in your opinions? Explain in the space provided.

Statement	Agree	Disagree	Undecided
1. If a person finds computers hard to use, it's because he or she isn't smart enough.			
2. For most people, having a wireless phone or pager is essential.			
3. Consumers should expect to replace high-tech products every two to three years to keep up with new technology.			
4. The more features and capabilities an electronic product has, the better.			
5. Since technology is constantly changing, consumers must rely on the recommendations of expert salespeople.			
6. Shopping for a wireless phone is confusing because so many different plans are offered.			
7. When different companies compete to provide local and long distance phone service, consumers benefit.			
8. The government should ensure that all citizens have access to the Internet.			
9. Whatever type of computer is used by the majority of people must be the best choice.			
10. A used computer might meet a consumer's needs just as well as a new one.			

Answers changed: _____

Why? _____

_____

_____

_____

Chapter 17 Technology Products

Study Guide

Directions: As you read Chapter 17, answer the following questions. Later you can use this study guide to review chapter information.

Section 17.1 Managing Technology Choices

1. What is the purpose of planned obsolescence? How might the strategy backfire? _____
   _____
   _____
   _____
   _____
   _____
   _____

2. How can you determine if you're ready for a new product? _____
   _____
   _____

3. What are two possible advantages of waiting a few months before buying a brand new technology product? _____
   _____
   _____
   _____

4. What research can you do before shopping for a new technology product? _____
   _____
   _____
   _____
   _____

5. What are two disadvantages of choosing products with extra features? _____
   _____
   _____
   _____

Section 17.2 Choosing Phone Service

6. From a consumer standpoint, what is the difference between analog and digital phone service?
   _____
   _____
   _____
   _____

(Continued on next page)

7. What are two advantages of using prepaid telephone service? _____

_____

_____

_____

8. What happens if you use more minutes of phone usage in a month than you signed up for?

_____

_____

_____

_____

9. When do you incur roaming charges? _____

_____

_____

_____

10. What features should you check when shopping for a phone? _____

_____

_____

_____

11. Describe two ways you can show courtesy when using a wireless phone. _____

_____

_____

_____

_____

12. Why is it advisable to sign up for a specific phone service rate plan? _____

_____

_____

_____

13. How would you know if you were a victim of cramming? _____

_____

_____

_____

Section 17.3 Choosing Internet Service

14. What are three possible drawbacks of dial-up access to the Internet? _____

_____

_____

_____

_____

_____

15. Identify three ways that users can get broadband Internet access. _____

_____

_____

_____

_____

16. What factors should you research when comparing Internet service providers? _____

_____

_____

_____

_____

17. How can consumers get access to the Internet while traveling? _____

_____

_____

_____

_____

(Continued on next page)

Section 17.4 Choosing a Home Computer

18. Name three advantages that desktop computers have over laptops. _____
_____
_____
_____
_____

19. What factors do you need to consider when comparing computer systems? _____
_____
_____
_____

20. Why is the amount of RAM a computer has an important consideration? _____
_____
_____
_____
_____
_____

21. What does a typical computer software package include? _____
_____
_____
_____
_____

22. What is shareware? How do you pay for it? _____
_____
_____
_____
_____

23. Identify four low-cost alternatives to buying a new computer. _____
_____
_____
_____
_____

Chapter 17 Technology Products

Trying Technology

Directions: Read the following story and answer the questions that follow.

The Williams family has had some problems with technology lately. Their computer, which is just over a year old, recently stopped working. Because the family purchased an extended service agreement, they have a three-year warranty on the computer. After four attempts at replacing parts to repair the computer, the technician determined that the computer could not be fixed. Mrs. Williams thought the manufacturer would refund the $1,300 she paid for the computer last year, but instead she received a new computer model with upgraded features. The new computer retails for $799.

Without a computer and the Internet for a month, Aaron, age sixteen, and Angie, age fifteen, had to stop chatting with their friends online. As a result, they began to use the telephone more often. Now that their Internet service has been restored, they find that trying to use the telephone is frustrating because the phone line is often tied up with the computer. Aaron wants to buy a wireless phone. He has volunteered to pay the activation fee for the wireless phone with earnings from his part-time job.

1. If you were Mrs. Williams, would you be upset that you were given a $799 computer to replace your $1,300 computer? Why or why not? Why would the price have dropped so dramatically?

   _____
   _____
   _____
   _____
   _____
   _____
   _____
   _____

2. Other than buying a wireless phone, what options might the family investigate so they could make and receive phone calls while someone was logged onto the Internet?

   _____
   _____
   _____
   _____
   _____
   _____
   _____
   _____

(Continued on next page)

3. What is the drawback to Aaron's offer to pay the activation fee for wireless phone service?

_____

_____

_____

_____

_____

4. If the family decided to invest in a wireless phone, what questions should they ask themselves about how it would be used? Would they be wise to select a plan with limited airtime in order to save money?

_____

_____

_____

_____

_____

_____

_____

_____

_____

5. The Williams' new computer has a convenient port for a digital camera. Before buying a digital camera, what steps would you suggest that the family take?

_____

_____

_____

_____

_____

_____

_____

_____

_____

Chapter 18 Clothing and Grooming

Attitude Inventory

Directions: Before you begin Chapter 18, take stock of your attitudes by completing the following inventory. Read each statement and check the appropriate column to indicate whether you agree, disagree, or are undecided. Use the space provided at the bottom of the page to write your comments about at least three of the statements. You will refer to this page again after completing your study of the chapter.

Statement	Agree	Disagree	Undecided
1. Clothing purchases should be based on knowing what clothing you already have.			
2. "Never throw clothing out—it's bound to come back in style" is good advice.			
3. Clothing styles are only as good as they look on you.			
4. When purchasing clothing, always choose the best quality available.			
5. Used clothing should be purchased only as a last resort.			
6. The price tag on a clothing item is generally the best indicator of quality.			
7. Most people today would rather buy new clothing than repair the clothing they have.			
8. Most machine-washable items can be washed together in one load to save time and energy.			
9. Different brands of grooming products vary a great deal in quality.			
10. I would be willing to pay extra for a shampoo labeled "all natural."			

Comments: _____

_____

_____

_____

_____

_____

_____

(Continued on next page)

 **Attitude Inventory** *(Continued)*

Rechecking Your Attitude

Directions: After completing your study of Chapter 18, respond to the Attitude Inventory statements a second time. Then compare your two sets of responses. Use the space provided at the bottom of the page to note which of your answers changed. What do you think accounts for these shifts in your opinions? Explain in the space provided.

Statement	Agree	Disagree	Undecided
1. Clothing purchases should be based on knowing what clothing you already have.			
2. "Never throw clothing out — it's bound to come back in style" is good advice.			
3. Clothing styles are only as good as they look on you.			
4. When purchasing clothing, always choose the best quality available.			
5. Used clothing should be purchased only as a last resort.			
6. The price tag on a clothing item is generally the best indicator of quality.			
7. Most people today would rather buy new clothing than repair the clothing they have.			
8. Most machine-washable items can be washed together in one load to save time and energy.			
9. Different brands of grooming products vary a great deal in quality.			
10. I would be willing to pay extra for a shampoo labeled "all natural."			

Answers changed: _____

Why? _____

_____

_____

_____

_____

_____

Chapter 18 Clothing and Grooming

Directions: As you read Chapter 18, answer the following questions. Later you can use this study guide to review chapter information.

Section 18.1 Planning Clothing Purchases

1. Identify three physical factors that influence clothing decisions. _____
   _____
   _____

2. Why do you need to figure out what kinds of clothes are right for you? _____
   _____
   _____
   _____

3. List six social factors that might influence your clothing decisions. _____
   _____
   _____
   _____

4. When assessing your wardrobe, what should you do with items you no longer want? _____
   _____
   _____
   _____

5. How does focusing on two or three colors help stretch your wardrobe? _____
   _____
   _____
   _____
   _____

Section 18.2 Shopping for Clothing

6. What is the difference between a department store and a specialty store? _____
   _____
   _____
   _____

(Continued on next page)

7. What is the advantage of shopping at an outlet store? What is one possible disadvantage?

_____

_____

_____

8. When buying clothes that are on sale, why should you find out if the sale is final?

_____

_____

_____

9. What should you do when trying on a garment to make sure it fits? _____

_____

_____

_____

10. Name the three main types of fibers. _____

_____

_____

11. How are woven fabrics different from knitted fabrics? Which is the stronger fabric?

_____

_____

_____

_____

12. What information is required by law to be on a garment's labels? _____

_____

_____

_____

Section 18.3 Caring for Clothing

13. Identify three advantages of putting clothes away properly when you are not wearing them.

_____

_____

_____

14. Why is it important to sort dirty clothes before washing them by machine? _____

_____

_____

_____

15. For what kinds of fabrics is hand washing advised? _____

_____

_____

16. What is the difference between ironing and pressing? _____

_____

_____

_____

_____

17. What are two advantages of making a simple repair on a garment as soon as you see that it is needed? _____

_____

_____

_____

18. Why is it important to clean or wash all clothes before putting them away for the off season?

_____

_____

_____

Section 18.4 Choosing Grooming Products

19. How are the laws covering grooming products different from those covering drugs? _____

_____

_____

_____

(Continued on next page)

20. How can you tell if a particular grooming product is regulated as a drug? _____
    _____
    _____
    _____
    _____

21. What should you keep in mind about the term *dermatologist-tested* on the label of a grooming
    product? _____
    _____
    _____
    _____

22. Why do some manufacturers use prestige pricing on grooming products? _____
    _____
    _____
    _____
    _____

23. What's the first safety precaution you should take before using any grooming product?
    _____
    _____
    _____
    _____

Name_____ Date_____ Class _____

Activity

Clothes for Campus

Directions: Jim has just graduated from high school and will be going on to college. Over the summer he grew two inches and none of his clothes fit. He needs a new wardrobe to take with him to school. In the space provided, plan a mix-and-match wardrobe for Jim that follows these guidelines:

- You must choose from the items listed in the left column below.
- You can select as many of each item as you think is appropriate.
- The wardrobe must include at least 10 pieces.
- You must stay within an $800 budget, including 6% sales tax.
- Jim will work at a restaurant three nights a week. On the job, he must wear black slacks and a white dress shirt.
- The weather will be cold in winter, and Jim must walk to class.

After planning Jim's wardrobe, complete the item on the next page.

Wardrobe Options

Item	Price
Suit	$399.95
Blazer	$89.95
Flannel Shirt	$19.99
Dress Shirt	$24.95
Casual Shirt	$22.99
Hooded Sweatshirt	$39.95
Sweat Pants	$25.95
Slacks	$39.95
Jeans	$39.95
Denim Jacket	$59.95
Dress Shoes	$69.95
Casual Shoes	$49.99
Tie	$19.95
Belt	$24.95
Sweater	$59.95
Top Coat	$159.95
Casual Coat	$79.95
Gloves	$19.99
Knit Stocking Cap	$5.95

Your Choices

Item	Price
1.	
2.	
3.	
4.	
5.	
6.	
7.	
8	
9.	
10.	
Subtotal	
Add 6% Sales Tax	
TOTAL	

(Continued on next page)

In the space below, explain why the wardrobe you planned is appropriate for Jim.

_____

_____

_____

_____

_____

_____

_____

_____

_____

_____

_____

_____

_____

_____

_____

_____

_____

_____

Consumer Education & Economics Student Activity Manual
Copyright © Glencoe/McGraw-Hill

Chapter 18 Clothing and Grooming

Activity

Wardrobe Solutions

Directions: Assume that you are asked to help a younger brother or sister do a wardrobe inventory. What solutions would you recommend for each of the problems listed below?

1. Raincoat (no longer repels water): _____

_____

_____

2. Shoes (heels run down, hole in one sole, uppers good): _____

_____

_____

3. Jeans (bottoms frayed, fabric weakened and wearing through at the seams): _____

_____

_____

4. Winter coat (too small across the shoulders, too short): _____

_____

_____

5. Sweatshirt (poor color, sleeves and length too long): _____

_____

_____

6. Jacket (pocket ripped beyond mending, elbows worn through): _____

_____

_____

7. Sweater (solid blue, faded and stretched, but otherwise usable): _____

_____

_____

_____

8. Two tops, two pairs of shorts (all in good condition; from different sets, but poorly coordinated):

_____

_____

_____

9. Jogging suit/sweats (one year old, never worn; one size too large): _____

_____

_____

_____

 **Activity**

Chapter 18 Clothing and Grooming

Reading Care Labels

Directions: Study the clothing care labels shown below. Then answer the questions that follow.

Garment 1

60% RAYON
20% POLY
10% SILK
6% WOOL
4% FLAX
DRY CLEAN ONLY

Garment 2

70% COTTON – 30% RAYON
Hand wash in cool water with mild detergent. Rinse thoroughly, keeping water clear of excess dye. Do not use any cold water wool washes. Dry flat. No bleach. Cool iron.

Garment 3

100% Cotton
Hand Wash Cold.
Do Not Twist.
Reshape. Dry Flat.

Do Not Dry Clean.

Garment 4

100% POLYESTER
MACHINE WASH WARM DELICATE
TUMBLE DRY LOW
REMOVE PROMPTLY
COOL IRON

1. Which garment(s) are made from blends? _____

2. Which garment(s) are made from natural fibers exclusively? _____

3. Which garment(s) can be machine washed? _____

4. Which garment(s) must be hand washed? _____

5. Which garment(s) cannot be washed at all? _____

6. Which garment(s) can be washed in hot water? _____

7. Which garment(s) must be ironed using minimal heat? _____

8. What does the instruction "Dry flat" (as in labels 2 and 3) mean? Why do you think it is included?

_____

_____

9. Look at the label for garment 1. What is "poly"? What is flax? _____

_____

_____

10. Which garment(s) might fade or "run" when washed? How do you know? _____

_____

_____

Consumer Education & Economics Student Activity Manual
Copyright © Glencoe/McGraw-Hill

Chapter 19 Transportation

Directions: Before you begin Chapter 19, take stock of your attitudes by completing the following inventory. Read each statement and check the appropriate column to indicate whether you agree, disagree, or are undecided. Use the space provided at the bottom of the page to write your comments about at least three of the statements. You will refer to this page again after completing your study of the chapter.

Statement	Agree	Disagree	Undecided
1. An automobile is a necessity in most communities.			
2. Widespread ownership of automobiles presents problems for society.			
3. Public transportation is used mainly by those who don't have their own vehicle.			
4. Leasing a vehicle is almost always less expensive than buying one.			
5. Results of road tests reported by various magazines are of real value to the consumer.			
6. Dealer reputation is usually more important than the price of a car.			
7. The used-car buyer always "buys someone else's problem."			
8. It's rude to haggle over the price of a new car.			
9. Consumers have little defense against dishonest auto repair shops.			
10. Seatbelt use should be required for all drivers and passengers.			

Comments: _____
_____
_____
_____
_____
_____
_____
_____

(Continued on next page)

Rechecking Your Attitude

Directions: After completing your study of Chapter 19, respond to the Attitude Inventory statements a second time. Then compare your two sets of responses. Use the space provided at the bottom of the page to note which of your answers changed. What do you think accounts for these shifts in your opinions? Explain in the space provided.

Statement	Agree	Disagree	Undecided
1. An automobile is a necessity in most communities.			
2. Widespread ownership of automobiles presents problems for society.			
3. Public transportation is used mainly by those who don't have their own vehicle.			
4. Leasing a vehicle is almost always less expensive than buying one.			
5. Results of road tests reported by various magazines are of real value to the consumer.			
6. Dealer reputation is usually more important than the price of a car.			
7. The used-car buyer always "buys someone else's problem."			
8. It's rude to haggle over the price of a new car.			
9. Consumers have little defense against dishonest auto repair shops.			
10. Seatbelt use should be required for all drivers and passengers.			

Answers changed: _____

Why? _____

_____

_____

_____

_____

_____

Chapter 19 Transportation

Study Guide

Directions: As you read Chapter 19, answer the following questions. Later you can use this study guide to review chapter information.

Section 19.1 Transportation Options

1. Identify four benefits that individuals gain from using mass transit. _____
   _____
   _____
   _____
   _____

2. In what ways does the use of mass transit benefit society as a whole? _____
   _____
   _____
   _____

3. What actions have transit officials taken to reduce consumer resistance to using mass transit?
   _____
   _____
   _____
   _____
   _____
   _____

4. Identify the economic disadvantages of using one's own vehicle to get to work. _____
   _____
   _____
   _____
   _____

5. Why is it a good idea to talk to others who travel the same route when you are weighing transportation options? _____
   _____
   _____
   _____
   _____

(Continued on next page)

Section 19.2 Understanding Vehicle Financing

6. How does buying a vehicle differ from leasing one? _____

_____

_____

_____

_____

_____

7. When shopping for a loan, why do you need to consider the length of the loan as well as the interest rate? _____

_____

_____

_____

_____

_____

8. Why is it a good idea to make your down payment on a vehicle as large as possible? _____

_____

_____

_____

_____

_____

9. What questions do you need to ask yourself when deciding whether to lease or buy a vehicle?

_____

_____

_____

_____

_____

10. List the up-front costs you may have to pay when you lease a vehicle. _____

_____

_____

_____

_____

Section 19.3 Shopping for a Vehicle

11. Why is it important to consider your needs and wants before shopping for a vehicle? _____

_____

_____

_____

_____

12. Of the factors to consider when researching a vehicle, which ones might save you money in the

long run? _____

_____

_____

_____

13. What features should you examine when inspecting a used vehicle? _____

_____

_____

_____

_____

14. What features should you pay attention to when taking a vehicle for a test drive? _____

_____

_____

_____

_____

15. What should you do before signing any lease or purchase agreement? _____

_____

_____

_____

_____

16. What are lemon laws? What can you do if your vehicle turns out to be a lemon? _____

_____

_____

_____

_____

_____

(Continued on next page)

Section 19.4 Owning a Vehicle

17. What is a maintenance schedule? _____

_____

_____

_____

_____

18. Why is it advisable to get an estimate before you have a vehicle repaired? _____

_____

_____

_____

_____

_____

19. What is one way to save money if your vehicle needs to have parts replaced? _____

_____

_____

_____

_____

20. What should you do if you receive a recall notice? _____

_____

_____

_____

_____

21. Why should a person avoid making phone calls or eating while driving? _____

_____

_____

_____

_____

_____

_____

Chapter 19 Transportation

Activity

City Transit

Directions: Assume that the annual cost of operating the transit system of Center City is $412.7 million. Assume further that the transit system has 14,000 employees.

1. If revenue from passengers amounts to $174.6 million, how much of the operating budget must be subsidized by taxpayers? Show your calculation.

    _____

2. What percentage of the total budget is met by revenue? Show your calculation.

    _____

3. If federal and state governments contribute $20.4 million to the system, how much (in dollars) of the operating budget must be met by local government? Show your calculation.

    _____

4. If transit employees earn a total of $278 million each year, what is their average annual wage? Show your calculation.

    _____

5. For each of the Center City residents listed in the table below, compute the extra cost of driving to work each day instead of taking the bus. Complete the blank spaces in the table.

| Resident | Cost of Driving | | | | | Difference |
	Miles Traveled One Way	Auto Cost per Mile	Daily Parking Cost	Total Driving Cost	One-Way Bus Fare	
Kurtz	5	26.3¢	$5	$	$ .95	$
Desiderio	8	23.5¢	$2	$	$ .75	$
Loomis	15	25.8¢	$7	$	$1.65	$
Frankel	24	27.8¢	$8	$	$2.25	$

(Continued on next page)

6. Many communities make special transportation arrangements for those who physically cannot drive a car. Often these arrangements include a dial-a-ride service using vans equipped with lifts. Because of the special vehicles, the lack of planned routes, and the time required to help passengers board, such a service is expensive to operate. Consider the figures at the right for one community's program.

Passengers carried	22,266
Total vehicle miles driven.	87,132
Total vehicle hours operated.	8,296
Total operating cost	$122,304
Total income from passengers.	$37,218
Amount funded by taxes	$85,086

Using these figures, compute the following. Show your calculations.

a. Cost per vehicle mile: _____

b. Cost per vehicle hour: _____

c. Cost per passenger carried: _____

d. Average fare: _____

e. Cost to taxpayers per mile: _____

7. If you were arguing in support of a dial-a-ride program for your community, which of the above figures would you cite? In what context? What other figures might you want to have for the sake of comparison?

_____
_____
_____
_____
_____
_____
_____
_____

Consumer Education & Economics Student Activity Manual
Copyright © Glencoe/McGraw-Hill

Chapter 19 Transportation

Activity

Buying a Used Vehicle

Directions: You've narrowed down your search to what seems to be the ideal vehicle for you. It's four years old, gets good gas mileage, and has received high marks for safety and reliability. You have found two for sale in your area—one at a reputable dealer's lot and one being sold by an individual. Study the ads below and answer the questions that follow.

REPRISE Coupe 383, 4 yrs. old, red, 57,000 miles, very nice, power windows and locks, AC, CD player, very clean, one owner, $12,900, 555-1234, ask for Dawn.	REPRISE COUPE 383, 4 yrs. old, silver blue, loaded with options, excellent condition, well maintained, new tires, only 63,000 miles! $14,500. Tim's Auto Mart, 555-5678

1. How could you determine whether the asking price was fair? _____

   _____

   _____

   _____

   _____

   _____

2. As you inspect each used vehicle, what will you look for? _____

   _____

   _____

   _____

   _____

   _____

   _____

   _____

   _____

   _____

   _____

(Continued on next page)

Buying a Used Vehicle *(Continued)*

3. Based on the ad, what might be the advantages of buying the Reprise from the private owner?

_____

_____

_____

4. Based on the ad, what might be the advantages of purchasing the Reprise from the used car dealer?

_____

_____

_____

_____

5. Assuming you inspected both cars and found no problems, which car would you prefer to purchase? Why?

_____

_____

_____

_____

_____

_____

6. Why is it important to make as large a down payment as you can afford?

_____

_____

_____

_____

7. Refer to Figure 19-5 on page 487 of the text. Assume that you decide to borrow $12,000 to pay for your Reprise. At an interest rate of 5%, how much would the total cost of the loan be for each of the following loan terms?

3 years: _____

4 years: _____

5 years: _____

Chapter 20 Recreation

Directions: Before you begin Chapter 20, take stock of your attitudes by completing the following inventory. Read each statement and check the appropriate column to indicate whether you agree, disagree, or are undecided. Use the space provided at the bottom of the page to write your comments about at least three of the statements. You will refer to this page again after completing your study of the chapter.

Statement	Agree	Disagree	Undecided
1. Most Americans have more time for recreation than did their parents and grandparents.			
2. Time not spent productively is wasted time.			
3. By definition, leisure time is unplanned.			
4. Recreational activities don't have to be expensive.			
5. It's important to wear the right clothing for recreational activities.			
6. Reading about your travel destination ahead of time takes the fun out of a vacation.			
7. "Leave your credit card at home" is poor advice for a vacationer.			
8. Travel agents will eventually disappear because they are no longer needed.			
9. Budget motels are suitable only for those who like to "rough it."			
10. It's better to pack too much for a trip than to be without something you need or want.			

Comments: _____

_____

_____

_____

_____

_____

_____

(Continued on next page)

Rechecking Your Attitude

Directions: After completing your study of Chapter 20, respond to the Attitude Inventory statements a second time. Then compare your two sets of responses. Use the space provided at the bottom of the page to note which of your answers changed. What do you think accounts for these shifts in your opinions? Explain in the space provided.

Statement	Agree	Disagree	Undecided
1. Most Americans have more time for recreation than did their parents and grandparents.			
2. Time not spent productively is wasted time.			
3. By definition, leisure time is unplanned.			
4. Recreational activities don't have to be expensive.			
5. It's important to wear the right clothing for recreational activities.			
6. Reading about your travel destination ahead of time takes the fun out of a vacation.			
7. "Leave your credit card at home" is poor advice for a vacationer.			
8. Travel agents will eventually disappear because they are no longer needed.			
9. Budget motels are suitable only for those who like to "rough it."			
10. It's better to pack too much for a trip than to be without something you need or want.			

Answers changed: _____

Why? _____

_____

_____

_____

_____

_____

Consumer Education & Economics Student Activity Manual
Copyright © Glencoe/McGraw-Hill

Chapter 20 Recreation

Study Guide

Directions: As you read Chapter 20, answer the following questions. Later you can use this study guide to review chapter information.

Section 20.1 Planning Your Leisure Time

1. Identify five possible benefits of taking time out for recreation. _____
   _____
   _____
   _____

2. In what ways does recreation contribute to your social health? _____
   _____
   _____
   _____

3. What factors do people need to consider when deciding how to spend their leisure time?
   _____
   _____
   _____
   _____

4. Why is it important to balance your recreational activities? _____
   _____
   _____
   _____

Section 20.2 Managing Recreation Expenses

5. Give four examples of public recreational facilities that might be found in a community.
   _____
   _____
   _____

6. What are the main differences between pubic and private recreational facilities? _____
   _____
   _____
   _____
   _____

(Continued on next page)

7. Summarize the factors to check when choosing a recreational facility. _____
_____
_____
_____

8. What do you need to find out before spending money on recreational equipment? _____
_____
_____
_____

9. What is the main guideline to remember about dressing for a particular activity? _____
_____
_____

Section 20.3 Planning a Vacation

10. Why is it a good idea to plan a vacation as far ahead as possible? _____
_____
_____
_____

11. List the factors to investigate when researching a vacation. _____
_____
_____

12. What costs do you need to include when budgeting for a vacation? _____
_____
_____
_____

13. How can you save money on food when on vacation? _____
_____
_____
_____

14. How can an Internet travel site help you to arrange a vacation? _____
_____
_____
_____
_____

Chapter 20 Recreation

Vacation Planning

Directions: Assume you're planning a vacation to a major city 1200 miles from where you live. You've been saving up for this vacation a long time and want to make the most of it. Your trip can last up to nine days, and you have a budget of $1600.

1. Study the options for transportation, lodging, entertainment, and food described below. Think about which options you'd like to include in your vacation plan.
2. Use the table on the next page to record your choices for each day of the trip and their cost.
3. Calculate the total cost of your vacation. If it's over $1600, you must modify your choices to stay within your budget. If it's under $1600, you can save the rest for your next trip or go shopping.
4. Answer the question at the bottom of the next page.

Transportation Options

a. Charter flight: special group rate, $249 round trip; minimum stay 7 nights.
b. Airline: $356 round trip; must stay over a Saturday night.
c. Bus: 29 hours each way; leaves at noon; $99 round trip.
d. Car: 3 days each way with overnight stops; unleaded gasoline averages $1.45 per gallon; your car gets 30 miles to the gallon.
e. Train: 27 hours each way; leaves at 10 A.M.; choice of two fares—coach (reclining seat), $265 round trip; private sleeping car, $856 round trip.

Lodging Options

a. Hastings Hotel: downtown hotel, older, but well maintained; near theaters, museums, and shopping district; $130 per night.
b. The Lighthouse: 65 miles from the city, water-front location; rooms small, no TV; private beach for guests; maximum stay 3 nights; $99 per night.
c. The Park Lloyd: newly built high-rise down-town hotel; rooms small but well furnished; 40 shops and boutiques, swimming pool, fitness center; $175 per night.
d. Treadway Motel: part of a national chain; near downtown; large rooms, swimming pool; $65 per night.

e. Vicarage Gate Inn: old town historic area; mansion converted into luxury inn; large rooms with many extras; $250 per night.

Food Options

a. Fast food: $20 per day
b. Casual (buffets, chain restaurants): $30 per day
c. Adventurous (a variety of unique dining experiences): $40 per day
d. Trendy (the hottest new restaurants): $60 per day
e. Luxury (gourmet food): $80 per day

Entertainment Options

a. Big league sport of your choice: games on Wednesdays, Fridays, and Saturdays; tickets $30.
b. Museum pass: $22; includes admission to art museum, science museum, aquarium, and wax museum; good for two consecutive days.
c. Guided all-day tour: includes major land-marks and historic sites; $24 (lunch on your own).
d. Theater: live performance with music, danc-ing, special effects; evenings except Mondays; tickets $85.
e. Thrills and Chills Theme Park: "The scariest rides in the world"; $45 per day for unlimited rides; closed Wednesdays.

(Continued on next page)

 **Vacation Planning (Continued)**

In the table below, identify your choices for each day and their cost.

- Your entire trip (including travel time) must last at least three days, but no longer than nine days.

- In the transportation column, draw an arrow (if necessary) to show how many days you will be traveling.

- You are limited to one transportation choice. Your lodging, food, and entertainment choices can vary from day to day.

	Transportation	Lodging	Food	Entertainment
Saturday				
Sunday				
Monday				
Tuesday				
Wednesday				
Thursday				
Friday				
Saturday				
Sunday				
TOTAL EXPENSES				

GRAND TOTAL COST: $ _____

Briefly explain how you managed to stay within your budget while getting maximum enjoyment from your vacation.

_____

_____

_____

_____

Chapter 21 Food and Nutrition

Attitude Inventory

Directions: Before you begin Chapter 21, take stock of your attitudes by completing the following inventory. Read each statement and check the appropriate column to indicate whether you agree, disagree, or are undecided. Use the space provided at the bottom of the page to write your comments about at least three of the statements. You will refer to this page again after completing your study of the chapter.

Statement	Agree	Disagree	Undecided
1. Most Americans know and follow guidelines for good nutrition.			
2. If a food tastes good, it can't be good for you.			
3. Pizza is nutritious.			
4. Making food choices that reduce the risk of cancer and heart disease is something to be concerned about later in life.			
5. When food prices go up, it's because farmers are trying to make more money.			
6. It's best to shop for groceries every few days.			
7. The more nutritious a food is, the more it costs.			
8. Store brand foods are usually poor in quality.			
9. The information provided on food labels is helpful to consumers.			
10. Most people tend to make better food choices when eating at home than when eating out.			

Comments: _____

_____

_____

_____

_____

_____

_____

_____

(Continued on next page)

Name_____ Date_____ Class _____

Rechecking Your Attitude

Directions: After completing your study of Chapter 21, respond to the Attitude Inventory statements a second time. Then compare your two sets of responses. Use the space provided at the bottom of the page to note which of your answers changed. What do you think accounts for these shifts in your opinions? Explain in the space provided.

Statement	Agree	Disagree	Undecided
1. Most Americans know and follow guidelines for good nutrition.			
2. If a food tastes good, it can't be good for you.			
3. Pizza is nutritious.			
4. Making food choices that reduce the risk of cancer and heart disease is something to be concerned about later in life.			
5. When food prices go up, it's because farmers are trying to make more money.			
6. It's best to shop for groceries every few days.			
7. The more nutritious a food is, the more it costs.			
8. Store brand foods are usually poor in quality.			
9. The information provided on food labels is helpful to consumers.			
10. Most people tend to make better food choices when eating at home than when eating out.			

Answers changed: _____

Why? _____

_____

_____

_____

_____

_____

Consumer Education & Economics Student Activity Manual
Copyright © Glencoe/McGraw-Hill

Chapter 21 Food and Nutrition

Study Guide

Directions: As you read Chapter 21, answer the following questions. Later you can use this study guide to review chapter information.

Section 21.1 Choosing Nutritious Foods

1. Identify five factors that might influence your food choices. _____
   _____
   _____

2. What are nutrients? Why do different people need different amounts of nutrients? _____
   _____
   _____
   _____
   _____

3. Why are carbohydrates important to good health? _____
   _____
   _____
   _____

4. Why do you need to include fats in your eating plan? _____
   _____
   _____
   _____

5. Which three nutrients are particularly important during the teen years? _____
   _____

6. Why is it important to vary your food choices? _____
   _____
   _____

7. Which are better for you—foods with high nutrient density or foods with low nutrient density?
   Why? _____
   _____
   _____
   _____

8. Summarize the benefits of daily physical activity. _____
   _____
   _____
   _____

(Continued on next page)

9. What nutrients do whole grain foods supply? Give three examples of whole grain foods.

_____

_____

Section 21.2 Planning Food Purchases

10. Why are convenience foods often more expensive than other processed foods? _____

_____

_____

11. What is the advantage of buying fresh foods when they are in season? _____

_____

_____

12. How can food preparation and cooking skills save you money? _____

_____

13. How does planning meals ahead of time save you money? _____

_____

_____

14. Why is it a good idea to shop for food only once a week? _____

_____

Section 21.3 Shopping for Food

15. Summarize the factors to consider when evaluating different food stores. _____

_____

_____

_____

16. What basic information is required by law on a food label? _____

_____

_____

17. What does the term *net weight* refer to? _____

_____

_____

_____

18. List the four main types of information found on a Nutrition Facts label. _____

_____

_____

_____

19. What kinds of foods carry grade labels? What are grade labels based on? _____

_____

_____

_____

_____

20. What is the unit price of an item? What does unit pricing enable you to do? _____

_____

_____

_____

21. Why is it a good idea to buy store brand products? _____

_____

_____

22. Identify three ways of shopping defensively. _____

_____

_____

_____

23. What should you look for when choosing fruits and vegetables? _____

_____

_____

_____

24. What should you look for when buying fish? _____

_____

_____

25. What do you need to remember about buying refrigerated and frozen foods? _____

_____

_____

_____

(Continued on next page)

Section 21.4 Eating Out

26. How can you determine if a restaurant meal will provide the nutrients you need? _____

_____

_____

27. List four strategies for avoiding eating too much in a restaurant that serves large portions.

_____

_____

_____

_____

28. Why are broiled or grilled foods a better choice than fried foods? _____

_____

29. Give one advantage and one disadvantage of ordering à la carte. _____

_____

_____

_____

30. List four strategies for controlling the costs of eating out. _____

_____

_____

_____

_____

31. What should you do about the bill if you eat out with friends at a restaurant that will not provide separate checks? _____

_____

_____

32. What is a gratuity or tip? What is the usual starting figure for a restaurant tip?

_____

_____

_____

_____

Chapter 21 Food and Nutrition

Activity

Evaluating Eating Habits

Directions: Use what you have learned about good nutrition to evaluate the eating habits of the two people described below and on the next page.

Marcia is 16 and extremely figure conscious. "I eat for my jeans," she explains with a laugh and a groan. "You would, too, if you knew what they cost me." Possibly her jeans are costing Marcia more than she realizes. Study her meals for one day, then answer the questions that follow.

Breakfast	Lunch	Dinner
Hard roll and low-sugar fruit spread Tea with lemon	Pineapple chunks (½ cup) Low-fat cottage cheese (½ cup) Diet soda	Peas, carrots, stewed tomatoes (½ cup each) Baked potato, plain (½ cup) Crackers Tea with lemon

1. How well did Marcia do at choosing enough nutritious foods from each food group? Explain.

_____

_____

_____

_____

_____

_____

2. How well did Marcia do at following the advice of the Dietary Guidelines for Americans as described in your textbook? Explain. _____

_____

_____

3. How can Marcia improve her food choices and manage her weight healthfully? _____

_____

_____

_____

_____

_____

(Continued on next page)

Consumer Education & Economics Student Activity Manual
Copyright © Glencoe/McGraw-Hill

Jeff is 27 and an accountant. He is also overweight. "I can't figure it out," he complains. "I exercise twice a week, eat right, have all the things you're supposed to — meat, vegetables, milk. I even snack healthy — nothing but fruit between meals. And still I'm overweight. How come?" Study Jeff's three typical meals and see if you can help him.

Breakfast	**Lunch**	**Dinner**
Oatmeal with butter and syrup Ham and three-egg omelet Blueberry muffin Milk	Double cheeseburger (with pickle and ketchup) French fries (large order) Vanilla shake	Fried chicken (half) Mashed potatoes Corn (1 ear) Dinner rolls (2) Chocolate cake
Midmorning Snack	**Evening Snack**	
Canned peaches	Banana, Milk	

4. How well did Jeff do at choosing enough nutritious foods from each food group? Explain. _____

_____

_____

_____

_____

5. How well did Jeff do at following the advice of the Dietary Guidelines for Americans as described in your textbook? Explain. _____

_____

_____

_____

_____

_____

6. How can Jeff improve his food choices and manage his weight healthfully? _____

_____

_____

_____

_____

Chapter 21 Food and Nutrition

Activity

Unit Prices

Directions: Unit pricing and product labeling can help shoppers choose between items that would otherwise be difficult to compare. Read the following situation, then complete the items as directed.

You need approximately two cups of corn for a recipe. In terms of taste and preparation, it makes no difference to you whether the product is canned or frozen. Here are your options:

CANNED CORN	Size (oz.)	Price ($)	Unit Price (¢ per oz.)
National brand	15.25	.65	
Regional brand	15.25	.65	
Store brand	15.25	.50	
Gourmet brand	11	.79	

FROZEN CORN	Size (oz.)	Price ($)	Unit Price (¢ per oz.)
National brand	10	1.45	
Regional brand	16	1.15	
Store brand	16	.69	
Gourmet brand	16	1.49	

1. Without knowing the unit prices, what difficulties do you face in determining which product is the best buy?

   _____

   _____

   _____

2. Complete the charts above by computing the unit prices.

3. Which option is the best buy? _____

4. What factors do you think account for this result? _____

   _____

   _____

   _____

   _____

   _____

   _____

   _____

Activity

Chapter 21 Food and Nutrition

Nutrition Facts

Directions: Shown below is the Nutrition Facts label from a soup mix. Study the label, then use it and your textbook to answer the questions that follow.

1. If you prepared the entire package of soup mix and ate half of it, how many calories would you get from the soup? How many grams of fat? Explain how arrived at your answer.

   _____

   _____

   _____

   _____

2. What is the meaning of the figure "28%" listed next to sodium? Why is this information included on the label?

   _____

   _____

   _____

   _____

3. If the label did not provide the 28% figure referred to above, could you calculate that figure yourself using other information on the label? Explain.

   _____

   _____

   _____

   _____

Nutrition Facts		
Serving Size 1.5 oz.		
(42g / About 1/4 package)		
Servings Per Container about 4		
Amount Per Serving		
Calories 110	**Calories from Fat** 20	
		% Daily Value*
Total Fat 2 g		**3%**
Saturated Fat 1 g		**6%**
Trans Fat 0 g		
Cholesterol 5 mg		**2%**
Sodium 680 mg		**28%**
Total Carbohydrate 19 g		**6%**
Dietary Fiber 1 g		**2%**
Sugars 2 g		
Protein 3 g		

Vitamin A	4%	Vitamin C	15%
Calcium	6%	Iron	2%
Thiamin	4%	Folic Acid	6%

*Percent Daily Values are based on a 2,000 calorie diet. Your daily values may be higher or lower depending on your calorie needs:

	Calories	2,000	2,500
Total Fat	Less than	65 g	80 g
Sat Fat	Less than	20 g	25 g
Cholesterol	Less than	300 mg	300 mg
Sodium	Less than	2,400 mg	2,400 mg
Total Carbohydrate		300 g	375 g
Dietary Fiber		25 g	30 g

Calories per gram:
Fat 9 • Carbohydrates 4 • Protein 4

4. Would you consider this soup a good source of Vitamin C? Why or why not?

   _____

   _____

5. Suppose your daily calorie needs were 2,500 calories. According to the label, what would be your Daily Value for total fat? What percentage of that value would one serving of the soup provide?

   _____

   _____

Name_____ Date _____ Class _____

Chapter 22 Health Care

Directions: Before you begin Chapter 22, take stock of your attitudes by completing the following inventory. Read each statement and check the appropriate column to indicate whether you agree, disagree, or are undecided. Use the space provided at the bottom of the page to write your comments about at least three of the statements. You will refer to this page again after completing your study of the chapter.

Statement	Agree	Disagree	Undecided
1. Your health is your doctor's responsibility.			
2. It's not possible to avoid stress completely.			
3. Tobacco and alcohol use among teens is a serious problem.			
4. If a drug is sold over the counter, it can't harm you.			
5. Any weight loss product is worth a try.			
6. Natural herbal supplements can be dangerous.			
7. Most people don't need to see a doctor unless they are sick or injured.			
8. Consulting the Yellow Pages is probably the best way to select a doctor.			
9. Affordable child care should be more widely available.			
10. People who put their aging parents in a nursing home are selfish.			

Comments: _____

_____

_____

_____

_____

_____

_____

_____

_____

(Continued on next page)

Rechecking Your Attitude

Directions: After completing your study of Chapter 22, respond to the Attitude Inventory statements a second time. Then compare your two sets of responses. Use the space provided at the bottom of the page to note which of your answers changed. What do you think accounts for these shifts in your opinions? Explain in the space provided.

Statement	Agree	Disagree	Undecided
1. Your health is your doctor's responsibility.			
2. It's not possible to avoid stress completely.			
3. Tobacco and alcohol use among teens is a serious problem.			
4. If a drug is sold over the counter, it can't harm you.			
5. Any weight loss product is worth a try.			
6. Natural herbal supplements can be dangerous.			
7. Most people don't need to see a doctor unless they are sick or injured.			
8. Consulting the Yellow Pages is probably the best way to select a doctor.			
9. Affordable child care should be more widely available.			
10. People who put their aging parents in a nursing home are selfish.			

Answers changed: _____

Why? _____

_____

_____

_____

_____

_____

_____

_____

Chapter 22 Health Care

Directions: As you read Chapter 22, answer the following questions. Later you can use this study guide to review chapter information.

Section 22.1 Protecting Your Health

1. List four health habits that contribute to wellness. _____
_____
_____
_____

2. What are four techniques for managing stress? _____
_____
_____
_____

3. Why is it important to keep things in perspective at times of stress? _____
_____
_____
_____

4. Give one reason why car accidents are the biggest cause of injuries to teens. ____
_____
_____
_____
_____

5. Why is it important to know the risks involved with an activity? _____
_____
_____
_____

6. Identify three types of substances that harm your health and that are best avoided.
_____
_____

(Continued on next page)

Section 22.2 Buying Health Care Products

7. What is the main difference between prescription drugs and over-the-counter drugs?

_____

_____

_____

_____

_____

8. What information should you read before taking any medication? _____

_____

_____

_____

_____

9. What are side effects? Why do you need to know about the possible side effects of a drug?

_____

_____

_____

_____

_____

10. What are your two main options for getting a prescription filled? _____

_____

_____

_____

11. Why do you need to be cautious about using dietary supplements? _____

_____

_____

_____

_____

12. Why should you be wary of a product that claims to treat a disease for which there is no conventional treatment? _____

_____

_____

_____

Chapter 22 Health Care

Section 22.3 Using Medical Services

13. What is the difference between a primary care physician and a specialist? _____
_____
_____

14. What is the advantage to patients of using a physician who is in private practice? _____
_____
_____

15. What are the advantages to physicians of working in a group practice? _____
_____
_____

16. List the topics you need to ask about when choosing a health care provider. _____
_____
_____
_____
_____
_____

17. What information should you write down before seeing a health care provider? _____
_____
_____
_____
_____
_____
_____

Section 22.4 Child and Adult Care Services

18. How does corporate child care benefit both employers and employees? _____
_____
_____
_____

(Continued on next page)

19. What must a child-care establishment do to receive a license? _____

_____

_____

_____

20. List six factors that parents should consider when choosing a child-care facility.

_____

_____

_____

_____

_____

_____

21. What kinds of facilities are generally offered to people who live in retirement communities?

_____

_____

_____

_____

_____

22. Why might a continuing care facility be particularly suitable for an elderly married couple?

_____

_____

_____

_____

_____

Consumer Education & Economics Student Activity Manual
Copyright © Glencoe/McGraw-Hill

Chapter 22 Health Care

The Truth About Tanning

Directions: Read the following paragraphs, then use the information to answer the questions that follow.

Have you noticed magazine ads for sunlamps and tanning beds? The models in the ads look great—tanned, smiling, and healthy. Having a great tan may sound appealing now, but research shows that skin damage can occur from the use of such products.

Sunlamps and tanning beds give off ultraviolet (UV) radiation. The radiation causes you to tan, but it's also harmful to skin cells. If you use indoor tanning devices, you're adding to the radiation you already get from the sun. Over a lifetime, you can accumulate too much radiation. The result is an increased risk of skin cancer, premature skin aging, reduced immunity to diseases, skin and eye burns, cataracts, and blood vessel damage.

Some ads claim that only one type of ultraviolet radiation, called UVB, is harmful. They further claim that since their tanning devices emit only UVA rays, they are "safe." The truth, however, is that while UVA radiation does not cause sunburn, it's still suspected to cause skin cancer and other damage.

Even getting just a little bit of tan may not be safe. The next time you think about tanning, ask yourself whether you're willing to take the risks.

1. Why isn't a "safe" tan possible? _____

_____

_____

_____

2. What are some risks, other than cancer, from UV radiation? _____

_____

_____

_____

_____

3. What do you think is wrong with the following advertising claim? "Our modern facility uses advanced European UVA technology to provide you a safe, convenient, and beautiful tan."

_____

_____

_____

_____

_____

(Continued on next page)

4. What problems are each of the following FDA requirements designed to avoid? How effective do you think each requirement is in preventing problems? Why?

    a. Tanning salons must provide eye protection for customers.

    _____

    _____

    _____

    b. Tanning salons must use timers to limit customer exposure to UV lamps.

    _____

    _____

    _____

    _____

    _____

    _____

5. Why do you think tanning appeals to some people? Do you think their reasons for tanning are valid? Explain.

    _____

    _____

    _____

    _____

6. Suppose you were designing a public service campaign aimed at reducing the use of sunlamps and tanning beds. Describe the approach you would take.

    _____

    _____

    _____

    _____

    _____

    _____

    _____

    _____

Consumer Education & Economics Student Activity Manual
Copyright © Glencoe/McGraw-Hill

Chapter 22 Health Care

Weighing the Weight Loss Ads

Directions: Study the ads below. How are they promoting misconceptions about weight loss? Report your comments and concerns about the respective advertisements on the next page.

1

DON'T STARVE YOUR-SELF!

Lose 5 pounds a week while enjoying healthy, satisfying meals! Innovative eating plan provides a generous 1,200 calories a day.

"I'm so proud of my mom. She's lost 30 pounds and now we can even wear the same clothes!"
—Amy Smith, age 15

2

Special Internet Offer!!

Learn the age-old secret of the ancient Egyptians!

All-natural substance burns fat while you sleep!

Eat what you want when you want!

Order now! ABC Diet Pills are not available in stores.

Hurry, this is a limited-time offer.

3

Tired of weight loss plans that don't work?

Wouldn't it be great to eliminate shopping and cooking from your on-the-go lifestyle? Just follow this amazingly simple diet plan, eating our three nutritionally balanced, prepackaged meals and soothing shakes each day. You'll love the results! Guaranteed!

Special Offer for new clients only! Save $30 on food this month.

4

Swimsuit season's here, but are you...

Ashamed to go to the beach?

You can lose weight like the rich and famous do!!

Simply drink our specially formulated, fruit-flavored tonic for just 3 days and you'll be amazed at the results!

Say goodbye to those exercise videos and calorie counters!

(Continued on next page)

Weighing the Weight Loss Ads *(Continued)*

1. What techniques does Weight Loss Offer #1 use to entice potential customers? _____

_____

_____

What concerns do you have about Weight Loss Offer #1? _____

_____

_____

2. What techniques does Weight Loss Offer #2 use to entice potential customers? _____

_____

_____

What concerns do you have about Weight Loss Offer #2? _____

_____

_____

3. What techniques does Weight Loss Offer #3 use to entice potential customers? _____

_____

_____

What concerns do you have about Weight Loss Offer #3? _____

_____

_____

4. What techniques does Weight Loss Offer #4 use to entice potential customers? _____

_____

_____

What concerns do you have about Weight Loss Offer #4? _____

_____

_____

Name_____ Date_____ Class_____

Chapter 23 Housing and Furnishings

 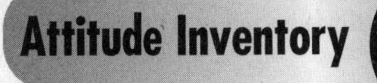

Directions: Before you begin Chapter 23, take stock of your attitudes by completing the following inventory. Read each statement and check the appropriate column to indicate whether you agree, disagree, or are undecided. Use the space provided at the bottom of the page to write your comments about at least three of the statements. You will refer to this page again after completing your study of the chapter.

Statement	Agree	Disagree	Undecided
1. Owning a home is an important part of "the good life."			
2. It's possible to buy a house, but not an apartment.			
3. A brief inspection of a rental unit is usually all that is needed before signing a lease.			
4. A person who rents an apartment has the right to privacy.			
5. Whether you're buying or selling a home, a real estate agent can be helpful.			
6. Prospective home buyers should determine the maximum they can afford and look for a home priced accordingly.			
7. It's important to completely furnish your first apartment as soon as possible after moving in.			
8. There is only one standard for judging upholstered furniture: is it comfortable?			
9. As long as you don't mind, there's nothing wrong with living in a messy home.			
10. The responsibility for cleaning and maintaining a home should be shared by everyone who lives in it.			

Comments: _____

_____

_____

_____

_____

_____

_____

_____

(Continued on next page)

 **Attitude Inventory (Continued)**

Rechecking Your Attitude

Directions: After completing your study of Chapter 23, respond to the Attitude Inventory statements a second time. Then compare your two sets of responses. Use the space provided at the bottom of the page to note which of your answers changed. What do you think accounts for these shifts in your opinions? Explain in the space provided.

Statement	Agree	Disagree	Undecided
1. Owning a home is an important part of "the good life."			
2. It's possible to buy a house, but not an apartment.			
3. A brief inspection of a rental unit is usually all that is needed before signing a lease.			
4. A person who rents an apartment has the right to privacy.			
5. Whether you're buying or selling a home, a real estate agent can be helpful.			
6. Prospective home buyers should determine the maximum they can afford and look for a home priced accordingly.			
7. It's important to completely furnish your first apartment as soon as possible after moving in.			
8. There is only one standard for judging upholstered furniture: is it comfortable?			
9. As long as you don't mind, there's nothing wrong with living in a messy home.			
10. The responsibility for cleaning and maintaining a home should be shared by everyone who lives in it.			

Answers changed: _____

Why? _____

_____

_____

_____

_____

_____

Chapter 23 Housing and Furnishings

Directions: As you read Chapter 23, answer the following questions. Later you can use this study guide to review chapter information.

Section 23.1 Housing Options

1. Give five examples of the kinds of facilities and services that might influence a person's choice of home. _____

_____

2. Identify five different types of single- and multiple-family dwellings. _____

_____

_____

3. What does condominium ownership involve? _____

_____

_____

4. In what ways does renting a home offer more flexibility than owning one? _____

_____

_____

_____

5. What advantages does owning a home have over renting one? _____

_____

_____

_____

Section 23.2 Renting a Home

6. What are the main sources of information about available rental units? _____

_____

_____

_____

(Continued on next page)

7. What is the purpose of preparing an inspection checklist before you inspect a rental unit?

_____

_____

_____

8. What is the purpose of the Fair Housing Act? _____

_____

_____

_____

9. What should you do before you sign a lease for a rental unit? _____

_____

_____

_____

10. What can you do if you disagree with any of the terms of a lease? _____

_____

_____

_____

11. Summarize the responsibilities you have as a tenant. _____

_____

_____

_____

12. Briefly describe the actions you should take when you move out of a rental unit. _____

_____

_____

_____

_____

Section 23.3 Buying a Home

13. List the continuing costs that are involved in home ownership. _____

_____

_____

_____

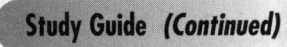
14. Why does a lender put extra funds from monthly payments into an escrow account?

_____

_____

15. What is the main disadvantage of an adjustable rate mortgage? _____

_____

_____

16. What are points? What does a point cost? _____

_____

17. What is a multiple listing service, or MLS? _____

_____

18. How do you go about making an offer on a home? _____

_____

_____

19. Give five examples of professional inspections that might be made on a home. _____

_____

_____

20. At what point does a sales contract on a home become legally binding? _____

_____

_____

Section 23.4 Furnishing a Home

21. What are the drawbacks of buying furniture through a "rent-to-own" agreement? _____

_____

_____

_____

_____

(Continued on next page)

22. What do you need to think about when developing a floor plan for a room? _____
_____
_____

23. What factors should you keep in mind when shopping for furniture? _____
_____
_____

24. Why do you need to note the size of large appliances when researching different models?
_____
_____
_____
_____

25. What factors should you consider when comparison shopping for a large appliance?
_____
_____
_____

Section 23.5 Maintaining a Home

26. Identify four benefits of keeping a home clean and in good repair. _____
_____
_____
_____

27. Identify three ways of reducing the amount of cleaning that needs to be done. _____
_____
_____

28. What does preventive maintenance involve? _____
_____
_____

29. What actions can you take to prevent fires in your kitchen? _____
_____
_____

30. What can you do to prevent carbon monoxide poisoning in your home? _____
_____
_____
_____

Chapter 23 Housing and Furnishings

Apartment Ads

Directions: Theo and Sharyl are hunting for an apartment. Below is a description of their situation and several apartment ads from the local newspaper. After reading the description and the ads, decide whether Theo and Sharyl should consider each apartment. Write either "Investigate further" or "Rule out" in the space provided and explain why.

Theo and Sharyl were married several months ago after meeting on the job at C&E Enterprises. They live in suburban Panorama with their cat and commute across town to Tolliver, where C&E is located. Because their car is old and inefficient, commuting is expensive. Theo and Sharyl feel that they cannot afford a new automobile. Instead, they are considering a move to shorten their commute.

Sharyl and Theo currently pay $425 a month for an unfurnished, two-bedroom apartment (utilities excluded). They can manage this amount easily since their combined take-home pay comes to about $600 a week. They have a joint checking account which contains $1,450 and savings of approximately twice that amount.

a. $75 wk. Immaculate. Furnd rms, some w/hot plates. Converted motel nr C&E Ent.

b. $400 plus utils, 2 bdrm, stv/frig. Off-st. pkg. Nr I-280 exit.

c. $575. TRINITY LANE Furnished Apts. Newly dec 2 bdrm, 1 ba. Laun., pkg., charmg garden. Lease & dpst reqd. Limit 1 child.

d. $400. 1 bdrm apt, upstrs pvt home. All util pd. Beau furnd. Share entr, laun. No pets, children, late hrs. Apply only if employd & mature. Refs reqd.

e. $450 up, 1 & 2 bdrm apts. Sec complex, elev bldgs, undergrnd pkg. Full kitchens, cpt/drps. Pool, gym, clubhse. Small pet OK w/dpst. Cnvnt locat nr bus & shopg.

a. _____

_____

_____

b. _____

_____

_____

_____

_____

c. _____

_____

_____

d. _____

_____

_____

e. _____

_____

_____

(Continued on next page)

Apartment Ads (Continued)

f. | $625 plus util. FAMILIES WELCOME! 3 bdrm, 2 ba. Cpts/drps, laun. Pool, playgrd, pkg.

g. | $785. Triplex penthse. Classic 2 bdrm & den, 2½ ba. Firepl, beam ceilgs, carport, balc. Quiet hillside locat, view.

PANORAMA

h. | $325. 2 rms, ba. Furnd. Utls pd.

f. _____
_____
_____
_____
_____

g. _____
_____
_____
_____

h. _____
_____
_____
_____

Chapter 23 Housing and Furnishings

Activity

Rental Agreement

Directions: The first page of a lease appears below. Study it, noting especially the restrictions on and duties of the tenant. Then answer the questions on the following page.

LEASE

This Agreement is made and entered into this 14th day of May, 20—, by and between Total Control Management Co. (hereinafter referred to as "Lessor") and Annie B. Student (hereinafter referred to as "Lessee"). WITNESSETH: That for and in consideration of the payment of rents and the covenants and obligations contained herein, Lessor does hereby lease to Lessee the premises known as Apartment #111 located at 14777 Portsmouth Place, Los Angeles, California. It is further mutually agreed between the parties as follows:

1. Lessor leases to Lessee the above described premises for a term of 1 year, beginning on June 1, 20—, and ending at 12 midnight on May 31, 20—.

2. Monthly rent of four hundred fifty dollars ($450.00) is due and payable on the 1st day of each month of the term, with first and last installments to be paid upon the execution of this agreement, and the second installment to be paid on July 1, 20—.

3. Upon execution of this agreement, Lessee shall deposit with Lessor the sum of four hundred fifty dollars ($450.00) as security for any damage caused to the premises during the term of lease. Such deposit shall be returned to Lessee, without interest, and less any amount for damages to the premises, within 30 days of termination of this agreement.

4. In the event that any payment required to be paid by Lessee hereunder is not made within three (3) days of when due, Lessee shall pay to Lessor, in addition to such payment or other charges due, a Late Fee in the amount of fifty dollars ($50.00).

5. Premises shall be used and occupied by Lessee only. Lessee shall not allow any other person, except transient relatives and friends who are guests of Lessee, to use or occupy the premises without first obtaining written consent from Lessor.

6. Lessee shall not keep or permit to be kept in said premises any dog, cat, bird, or other animal.

7. Lessee shall make no alterations, additions, or improvements to the premises without prior written consent of Lessor. All alterations, additions, or improvements made in or to the premises shall, unless otherwise provided by written agreement between Lessor and Lessee, be the property of Lessor and remain on the premises at the termination of this agreement.

8. Lessee shall not sublet the premises or any part thereof, or assign this agreement, without Lessor's written consent.

9. Lessee shall arrange and pay for all utility services supplied to said premises.

10. The cost of repairs for damages caused by Lessee, Lessee's guests, or persons under Lessee's control shall be paid for by Lessee; otherwise, the cost of repairs shall be paid by Lessor.

(Continued on next page)

1. What is the minimum amount of money it will cost Annie to move into her new apartment? Explain.

_____

_____

2. After moving in, Annie is short of cash, so she waits until she receives her paycheck on July 5 to make her next rent payment. How much does she owe at that time? Why?

_____

_____

3. To reduce expenses, Annie would like to share her apartment with a friend. According to her lease, can she? Why or why not?

_____

_____

4. Annie puts some corn husks down the garbage disposal, clogging the kitchen sink. She is unable to get it unclogged and calls a plumber. Who must pay for the plumber? Why?

_____

_____

_____

5. During a heat wave, the electric bill is double the usual amount. Who pays the increase? Why?

_____

_____

6. While browsing at a home improvement center one Saturday, Annie finds some wallpaper that she thinks would brighten up the kitchen. She purchases the wallpaper, puts it up that afternoon, and sends the sales receipt to the landlord. Do you think he will reimburse Annie for the cost of the wallpaper? Why or why not?

_____

_____

_____

_____

7. Annie wants more storage space, so she gets an okay from the landlord to build a shelf unit and attach it to a wall. She pays for the materials herself. When Annie moves out at the end of the lease period, can she take the shelf unit with her? Explain.

_____

_____

_____

_____

Chapter 23 Housing and Furnishings

Activity

Mortgage Math

Directions: David and Jennifer Chen are preparing to become homeowners for the first time. Use the information provided to complete each item as directed. Show your calculations.

1. A guideline used by some lenders is that housing expenses—including mortgage loan payments, property taxes, and home insurance—should total no more than 29% of gross income. According to this guideline, how much can the Chens afford to pay for housing each month if David earns $38,000 per year and Jennifer earns $46,000 per year?

   _____

   _____

2. David and Jennifer have saved $6,000 for a down payment. Disregarding other factors, what is the highest priced home they could afford based on a 5% down payment? (Hint: Home price × 0.05 = down payment amount.)

   _____

   _____

3. Besides income and savings, what other financial figure will lenders consider when prequalifying the Chens for a mortgage loan?

   _____

   _____

4. After reviewing their financial information, the lender gives the Chens a figure for the maximum amount they can afford to pay for a home. What else should David and Jennifer consider before telling their real estate agent what price range to look for?

   _____

   _____

   _____

   _____

5. A home is listed for sale at $95,000. If David and Jennifer purchased this home and made a 5% down payment, what would be the down payment amount? What would be the size of their mortgage?

   _____

   _____

   _____

   _____

   _____

(Continued on next page)

Mortgage Math *(Continued)*

Suppose David and Jennifer find a home they want to buy, and their offer of $110,000 is accepted. They decide to make a 10% down payment. Use the table below to answer the following questions. Show your calculations.

Monthly Principal and Interest for each $1,000 Borrowed			
Interest Rate	15 Years	20 Years	30 Years
4.00%	$7.40	$6.06	$4.77
4.50%	$7.65	$6.33	$5.07
5.00%	$7.91	$6.60	$5.37
5.50%	$8.17	$6.88	$5.68
6.00%	$8.44	$7.16	$6.00
6.50%	$8.71	$7.46	$6.32
7.00%	$8.99	$7.75	$6.65
7.50%	$9.27	$8.06	$6.99
8.00%	$9.56	$8.36	$7.34
8.50%	$9.85	$8.68	$7.69
9.00%	$10.14	$9.00	$8.05
9.50%	$10.44	$9.32	$8.41
10.00%	$10.75	$9.65	$8.78

Source: U.S. Department of Housing and Urban Development

6. If the Chens took out a 30-year loan at 7.00% interest, what would their monthly payment be?

_____

_____

7. If the Chens took out a 15-year loan at 6.50% interest, what would their monthly payment be?

_____

_____

8. Compare the loan options in items 6 and 7 above. Which loan would cost less in the long run? How much would the Chens save by choosing this loan?

_____

_____

_____

_____

Consumer Education & Economics Student Activity Manual
Copyright © Glencoe/McGraw-Hill